CO-FACILITATION

For my sons, Ben, and in memory
of his younger brother, Charlie, who gave
me so much joy throughout his short life.
You have both enriched my life beyond measure,
and beyond words.   J.K.

CO-FACILITATION

A PRACTICAL GUIDE TO USING PARTNERSHIPS IN FACILITATION

Joanna Knight and Warren Scott

**KOGAN
PAGE**

London ● Stirling (USA)

First published in 1997

Kogan Page Limited
120 Pentonville Road
London N1 9JN
and
22883 Quicksilver Drive
Stirling, VA 20166, USA

British Library Cataloguing in Publication Data

A CIP record for this book is available from the British Library.

ISBN 0 7494 2064 2

Typeset by Northern Phototypesetting Co Ltd, Bolton
Printed and bound in Great Britain by Biddles Ltd, Guildford and King's Lynn

Contents

Contents

1

Introduction and Background

WHY THIS BOOK?

The authors of this book are practitioners of consultancy; as a significant part of our work, we are involved in facilitating and enabling the development of groups of individuals and work teams. During the last few years, we have noticed a widespread shift in the way in which our colleagues in this field work with such groups. There has been a move away from training and tutor-led approaches, which tended to be fairly structured, focusing on a specific area of content, delivered by a subject expert to a passively receptive group who were dependent on the knowledge and understanding of the trainer. While individual and group learning undoubtedly occurred via these methods, and they remain appropriate in certain circumstances, their essential limitation is that learners do not learn how to learn for themselves. Because of major changes in both the public and private sectors, many organizations now want staff who are capable of managing in complex and changing situations, who feel empowered to make their own decisions without constant reference to authority, and who are active and continuous self-developers. Thus there has been a shift towards learner-centred approaches.

Such approaches have the advantage of focusing on the particular learning needs of group members, so that individual development is relevant and thus more likely to be transferred into the work environment. These needs are noted and responded to by a facilitator, who has responsibility for enabling the development of group members by focusing attention on their internal and interpersonal processes, how these act to enhance or inhibit their effectiveness, and helping to identify options for their further development. Group members are actively encouraged to take the major responsibility for their own development and for choosing whether and how to develop. In this way, group members are helped to learn how to learn and, ultimately, to become independent of the facilitator.

From our experience we know that while a trainer is apparently more active because of the obvious leadership role adopted, it is more demanding to act as facilitator. Although we often seem to do less when facilitating, we are observing the group and its members continually; considering what the issues seem to be for individuals, between individuals and for the group, and therefore what approaches might be effective; making decisions about whether, when and how to intervene; reviewing whether the activities in which the group is engaged are the most appropriate way of meeting the different learning needs; and retaining awareness of our own impact on group members so that this can be used to positive effect. This is not a definitive list. A number of people with whom we have worked on the development of their facilitation skills have noted and commented on the apparent paradox of the facilitative role, registering how demanding it has been to juggle so many balls at the same time.

We believe that one response to the demands of the facilitator role has been the growth in popularity of facilitators choosing to work together in their facilitation, that is to co-facilitate. Our research indicates that co-facilitation now forms a significant proportion, about half, of most facilitators' work. This is not due to inexperience or inability, since the facilitators involved in our research had an average of nine years' experience of working in this role. Their preference seems to be due to an acknowledgement that the demands of the role can better be met by co-facilitators, particularly if the work being undertaken is intensive.

We have become interested in co-facilitation as a direct result of our experiences in this field. Warren was involved over a period of time in what he experienced as an unsuccessful co-facilitative relationship, which remained difficult despite his best efforts to improve it. This made him realize the importance of being able to work effectively as a co-facilitator, and that his skills in this area were 'hit and miss'. Joanna's interest also derives from personal experiences which caused her to consider what made her co-facilitative relationships effective or not. On one occasion, she experienced difficulty in working with a co-facilitator with whom she had typically enjoyed a successful collaboration, but felt unclear as to why this difficulty had suddenly arisen. The following week she co-facilitated with two relatively new colleagues and felt conscious of both trusting and being trusted by them to facilitate the group-work effectively, though uncertain as to why this trust had arisen so quickly. This led her to explore co-facilitation in more depth.

We find it interesting, therefore, that while there is a range of programmes and workshops available to help practitioners to develop their facilitation skills, we do not know of any that specifically address the skills required in working effectively with another facilitator. Neither can we find much literature that focuses on co-facilitation itself – at best, it is a minor theme in a book or article on the art of facilitation. It therefore seems that little or no research has been undertaken into the subject of co-facilitation and what makes it effective or unsuccessful. Co-facilitation appears to be taken for granted, based on an assumption that if you can facilitate, you can co-facilitate. We know, from our own experience, that it is not so simple and straightforward an activity.

We have been fascinated by this taken-for-granted nature of co-facilitation and hope to challenge and change this. This book, and the research on which it is based, represents the first step into this particular territory. We hope that it will stimulate a trend towards a greater interest in the subject and greater awareness of the skills required for effective co-facilitation and the need actively to develop them.

THE RESEARCH BASE

Where does something begin and where does it end? Such distinctions are often arbitrary, based on our perceptions of external pressures and deadlines, rather than having any intrinsic meaning. It is certainly so with our research into co-facilitation. This research really started with our own experience as co-facilitators and our subsequent reflections on this, which led us to want to explore certain issues concerning co-facilitation in more depth. One research premise, based on our own experiences, was that co-facilitators who work effectively together pay good attention to how they initiate, build and maintain their working relationship in order to ensure its continued effectiveness. Our underlying assumption here was that effective co-facilitation is dependent on the existence of an effective relationship between the co-facilitators concerned. We also noticed how co-facilitation was often only addressed (if at all) when problems arose and were concerned to help ourselves and other co-facilitators to find ways of developing their abilities in addressing issues within their relationship *before* these had a negative or destructive impact on their working effectiveness.

Our formal, more purposeful research began as part of our work towards an MSc in Change Agent Skills and Strategies at Surrey University. Our prime purpose in undertaking this research was to find out about other practitioners' experiences of co-facilitation and to use the knowledge gained from this to inform and enhance future practice in co-facilitating. Our first action, having decided the particular focus of our inquiry and formulated our research plan, was to interview each other in order to uncover our experiences and thinking to date. These initial interviews helped us to identify some themes for the questionnaire we proposed to send out, and highlighted some of our underlying assumptions and biases, such as those referred to above.

In designing the questionnaire we wanted to encourage respondents to participate as fully as they felt able to, so we invited them to describe some specific experiences (both positive and negative) of co-facilitation and left plenty of room for comment in response to open questions.

The final questionnaire was sent out to a wide range of consultants, trainers and developers and academics, most of whom knew us directly. However, we attempted to ensure that the respondents were representative of both genders, differing ages and different roles – including external consultants, those employed in both the public and private sectors, academics and practitioners. In this way, we hoped to canvass a wide range of opinion and experience to give our conclusions greater applicability. This is particularly important as, during our literature review, we found no in-depth exploration of co-facilitation itself (as distinct from facilitation) and no evidence of any prior research undertaken in this area.

We were pleased to receive a number of unsolicited comments written on returned questionnaires, which indicated that people had found them interesting to complete:

'I thought the questionnaire was really quite thought-provoking and has given me an opportunity to learn a little more about my relationships and to evaluate their effectiveness.'

We were also pleased by the general willingness to become further involved in our research.

At this stage, we carried out an initial analysis of our research findings and began to identify some more significant themes that we were able to pursue during our interviews. We wanted to conduct interviews as part of our research in order to gain what Burgess (1982) has described as:

'the opportunity for the researcher to probe deeply to uncover new clues, open up new dimensions of a problem, and to secure vivid, accurate, inclusive accounts that are based on personal experience.'

Our intention was to help interviewees to 'search for and uncover the meaning of their experience' (Maclean, 1988). We therefore followed the interviewees' sense of what was important to them from their experiences of co-facilitation, although we had a general interview plan based on our early analysis. We noticed the degree of thoughtfulness of our interviewees, as indicated by periods of silence as they struggled to develop their thinking or were struck by a new perception about a particular experience, and by their ability to ask themselves probing questions in response to what they had just said – which relieved us of the desire or need to monopolize this role! We were again struck by the 'taken-for-granted nature of co-facilitation – as one interviewee explained, she'd never looked at *why* a particular co-facilitative relationship had worked before, she just knew that it had. It often seemed as though this was the first time that interviewees had reflected in any depth on their experiences of being a co-facilitator.

On one occasion two co-facilitators were interviewed together, giving us an opportunity not just to hear about their perceptions of their relationship but to experience and explore the dynamics between them as they happened. On another occasion both co-facilitators were interviewed separately, again allowing us to check out one perception of their relationship against the other partner's view. These interviews helped to assure us that we were gaining information about the reality of co-facilitation, rather than an espoused version.

After the interviews we again analysed our data, although this time in a more rigorous manner. We were concerned to do justice to the richness of the data and to use an holistic approach in analysing it, so we worked intuitively in identifying emerging themes and patterns and in testing out our emerging models. We tried to avoid the trap, which Easterby-Smith (1991) has identified, of attempting to quantify what is essentially qualitative information. We hope that, by this process, we have been able to generate what Gill and Johnson (1991) describe as inductive research: 'theory created or discovered through the observation of particular cases'.

Subsequently we have tried to test out our research conclusions by designing and running workshops for co-facilitators and by further reflections on our own ongoing co-facilitative experiences. This stage of the research process has involved the design and testing of the specific exercises, activities and reflections which are referred to at intervals throughout this book, and which are there to support readers who are practitioners of co-facilitation in improving their practice.

As we have already identified, the writing of this book gives an arbitrary sense of closure to our research process but does not mean that our informal thinking and experimentation in co-facilitation has stopped. We invite you to contact us with your critical reflections on the models, viewpoints, activities and experiences described in this book as one way of ensuring that this research continues and that our collective learning on this (to date) neglected subject grows.

Joanna Knight
Berkshire Consultancy Ltd
The Old Barn
Priory Court
Beech Hill
Reading RG7 2BJ
e-mail: Jo@berkshire.co.uk

Warren Scott
5 Taskers Lane
Burbage
Marlborough
Wiltshire
SN8 3TQ

2

Exploring Co-facilitation

This chapter sets out to define our understanding of co-facilitation and provides the foundation on which the rest of this book is based. Before attempting to offer a definition of co-facilitation, however, it is necessary to outline what we understand by facilitation as this inevitably informs our view of co-facilitation. We provide some practical examples of co-facilitation and highlight the difference between co-facilitation and simply working with someone else. Hopefully, you will see which elements of your experience fall within our understanding of co-facilitation and be able to identify others which fall outside our understanding of this term. This could help you to start thinking about how you might work with a co-facilitator (if you haven't previously worked in this way) or to consider when your practice as a co-facilitator has been effective and why.

In order to help you to recognize whether and to what extent you have so far been able to capitalize on the benefits of co-facilitation, and to avoid some of its more common pitfalls and limitations, we also describe both the advantages and the disadvantages of co-facilitation. Our research into the subject of co-facilitation showed that it is normally addressed as a minor theme of facilitation. Many explorations of co-facilitation confine themselves to little more than a list of the potential benefits and drawbacks, based on the authors' own experience rather than any wider research. We believe this book is the first attempt at a more in-depth exploration, drawing on research carried out with practitioners of co-facilitation, and supported and validated by our own experience. We hope that this fuller exploration will encourage you to maximize the benefits of your co-facilitative practice and to invest time, energy and attention in ensuring that you capture the benefits rather than experiencing the pitfalls.

FACILITATION: AN OVERVIEW

The term 'facilitation' is widely used among development practitioners, often in order to differentiate their approach and style from that of a trainer. However, sometimes it is used, it seems to us, without any precise or shared understanding of its meaning.

Some writers have provided useful descriptions of a facilitator, which serve to emphasize what we see as the important characteristics of facilitation. Heron (1989) describes a facilitator as 'a person who has the role of helping participants to learn in an experiential group'. Here he highlights the helping role of the facilitator and the desired outcome of that help, which is learning. We would define learning here as not just about the acquisition of new skills, attitudes or knowledge, but as about developing the ability to learn how to learn. Heron goes on to define an experiential group as one in which learning occurs through the active, conscious and holistic participation of its members. Such groups certainly represent one important forum in which facilitation takes place.

Further support for Heron's understanding of facilitation is provided by Spinks and Clements (1993): 'Facilitators are essentially enablers or encouragers of learning who seek to achieve this by focusing on the experiences and activity of the learner'. They reinforce the concept of learning as an active process and go on to differentiate facilitation from traditional didactic forms of teaching, in which learners are typically more passive – a common distinction. Again, Berry (1993) supports this understanding of facilitation, though she goes on to point out that it is practised in groups whose primary purpose is learning, and in action-oriented, more business-focused groups as well. This certainly supports our own experience, as we have often been asked to facilitate work groups in reaching shared and agreed business decisions as well as in their learning.

Berry also highlights another facet of facilitation: 'a willingness to take responsibility for the whole, seeking to enable each individual to contribute as appropriate'. This emphasizes the facilitator's role in relation to the group as well as the individual, highlighting what we see as the subtle interrelationship between the two and the need for the facilitator to pay simultaneous attention to both in order to help achieve the desired outcomes. It also stresses the fact that the facilitator does not have all the responsibility for the desired developmental outcomes, but that group members have an important role in contributing to the others' learning.

Throughout these descriptions there is an emphasis on the facilitator as an enabler, supporting group members in recognizing when, how and where their own or their colleagues' talents and experience might be useful and appropriate in helping the group, or individuals within it, to move forward towards the achievement of their desired outcomes. We believe that facilitators also offer frameworks or activities that can help in the achievement of these outcomes but that these are not imposed on group members, unlike in many forms of teaching or training, so that it remains group members' choice as to whether or not or how to utilize them. Because of this emphasis on enabling others and on offering guidance rather than overt leadership and strong direction, the role of facilitator can sometimes be perceived as essentially passive. In our experience, this is erroneous – as facilitators we may make fewer interventions than trainers, but we are constantly active in analysing the group and its individual members in terms of their progress towards their learning goals, what is happening, how this is aiding or inhibiting learning, what needs to change and how this could be affected and so on. In fact, the facilitator's role reminds us in some ways of a famous and often quoted view of leadership:

> 'A leader is best
> When people barely know he exists,
> Not so good when people obey and acclaim him,
> Worst when they despise him,
> But of a good leader, who talks little,
> When his work is done, his aim fulfilled,
> They will all say "We did this ourselves".'
>
> *Lao Tse, Chinese philosopher*

CO-FACILITATION: WHAT IS IT?

So, does co-facilitation simply refer to two or more people undertaking the activities and functions described above in working with a group? We were unable to find any definitions of co-facilitation in our reading on the subject. This implies that, having described the practice of facilitation, writers assume that their readers will automatically understand what is meant by any reference to co-facilitation. This assumption is questionable, however, since there seem to be different interpretations of the term to begin with, but it does reflect the 'taken-for-granted' nature of co-facilitation that we found through our research. Our intention is that our exploration of it here will prompt a reappraisal of its practice.

So, is co-facilitation simply what happens when two (or more) facilitators work together? How to define co-facilitation was an area of some disagreement between the practitioners whom we surveyed in our research. Some felt strongly that co-facilitation means two or more people are facilitating a group in its work – together and at the same time. For instance, we have worked together to facilitate many sessions where we have had equal responsibility for helping to achieve the desired outcome and for making appropriate interventions towards this. There has not been a designated 'lead facilitator' with the other one of us playing a supporting role. We have both been free to intervene as and when we saw fit, and leadership or initiative has moved from one to the other as it seemed relevant, depending on our knowledge, skill, inclination and so on.

Other facilitators involved in our research were of the view that if you facilitate different parts of the same programme or workshop, this also constitutes co-facilitation. However, this was termed 'co-training' by some, and seen as requiring lesser degrees of skill and coordination. Again, we have worked together on the design and delivery of programmes where we have consciously allocated leadership or a primary role in particular sessions to one of us, based on our understanding of the group's needs and our own skills and interests.

Essentially, we understand co-facilitation in the light of a whole programme or piece of work rather than one particular session. This seems to us to be a more inclusive understanding. We believe that the different notions of co-facilitation referred to above in fact describe different levels or degrees of coordination, rather than being intrinsically different activities. What is important is that co-facilitators share responsibility for helping the group and its members to achieve their aims, and for the way in which they achieve these. The distinguishing feature of co-facilitation is that it is intended to be a partnership, where two or more facilitators take joint responsibility for fulfilling the facilitation role. The purpose of this partnership is either to enable and maximize group and individual learning, or to help the group to achieve other ends such as making a business decision.

Gately and Gately (1993) describe co-teaching as a collaborative and equal relationship between two teachers, which creates a developmental process based on interaction and communication between the teachers involved. This suggests that, assuming co-facilitation has similar characteristics – and we believe it does – it can also enable the learning of the facilitators themselves, which would be highly congruent with their purpose of enabling learning for others. We have certainly found this to be true in our experience and know from our research that it has been a valuable aspect of co-facilitation for many others too. Any definition of co-facilitation therefore needs to reflect this important dimension which is a source of added value for co-facilitators themselves.

Putting all this together then, our working definition of co-facilitation is:

> Two or more facilitators working *in partnership* to enable a *group and its individual members* to reach an agreed outcome in a way that *maximizes* their own and others' *learning*, through the *active involvement* of all.

Although our understanding of co-facilitation is a broad one, incorporating both shared and individual leadership of particular sessions, we would not consider that guest speakers or other facilitators without shared responsibility for the whole enterprise were co-facilitators.

REFLECTION

▶ How would you define co-facilitation? Which aspects of our definition do you agree/disagree with?
▶ Does this definition help you to reflect on your practice as a co-facilitator? If so, in what ways?
▶ How might this definition help you to develop your co-facilitation in future?

THE ADVANTAGES OF CO-FACILITATING

The potential advantages of co-facilitating fall into two main areas:

● those concerning the facilitators themselves;
● those concerned with the effect on the group and the desired outcome of the work being undertaken.

We shall examine both types of advantage here. Of course, anything which has a positive effect on the group members is likely in turn to impact positively on the co-facilitators. For example, good feedback about their work will increase their chance of being asked to undertake more work in that organization or with similar groups. Similarly, if the co-facilitators feel positive benefits from working together, we suggest that this feeling is likely to enhance their capacity and capability to work well and may help deliver improved benefits for the group they are working with. In other words, the effect of any one advantage is likely to be multiplied.

It is worth noting that all these advantages are potential, in that co-facilitators have to work well together to capitalize on them. Later chapters in this book will provide you with ideas, activities and models to help you to achieve these benefits when co-facilitating.

Reduced risk of facilitator burn-out

From our own experience and our research, we know that many co-facilitators feel better able to withstand the pressure of undertaking their work when they are working alongside a trusted colleague. Although facilitation can appear easy to the untrained eye, it actually involves paying attention at many different levels – for example, to yourself, to individual group members, to what is being said and left unsaid, to the environment, to energy levels, to what interventions may best help at any particular point in time, to what progress is being made and to where blockages exist. One of the advantages of sharing responsibility for this work is that you are not the only person paying attention to all these issues. If you do not notice something or cannot think of an appropriate intervention, your co-facilitator is there alongside you working to achieve the same outcomes and may be more alert to what is happening and what is required on this occasion. One of the many ways of inhibiting effectiveness is self-induced pressure to perform, so just knowing that there is someone sharing this responsibility can enhance your contribution.

The work of facilitation can be very intense, as people engaged on their own development confront painful blockages or difficulties in their interpersonal relationships. Working with a co-facilitator can help to relieve this intensity or enable you to cope better with it. For instance, if one co-facilitator has been engaged in dealing with some very challenging issues with the group and has encountered some deep-seated resistance, they may temporarily feel quite tired and would welcome taking a lower profile role or not being present in the next session. This can allow them to recover their energy and full effectiveness, while the groupwork continues. In this way, you and your co-facilitator can pace yourselves, both during that particular piece of work and over a longer time period.

An example from our experience may help to highlight this particular benefit. Joanna was co-facilitating with a colleague, Sheila, on a long-term development programme for in-company trainers and consultants. At times, the group split into two action learning sets, each supported by one of the facilitators. In Sheila's set there was an individual who regularly acted in a very aggressive way with his colleagues, who were reluctant to give him feedback because of his capacity to undermine and attack them. Sheila frequently found herself needing to confront this person's behaviour and being on the receiving end of vitriolic personal attacks. Joanna, because of her lesser involvement with this individual, was able to provide Sheila with a high degree of support – at a personal level and by discussing options for dealing differently with the situation. This helped to give Sheila the strength to continue to challenge this person's behaviour, until his colleagues were able to deal with it for themselves – and the situation was finally resolved.

Provision of additional cover

If one facilitator is temporarily unable to function to their full capacity with the group, or suddenly has to leave the group to attend to urgent family or work business, for example, then co-facilitating means that disturbance to the work being undertaken is minimized. Another facilitator who has knowledge of the work, the desired outcomes, the group members and their history is in place ready and able to continue. This is a highly practical point, especially when people have come together to engage in work often at significant cost to themselves and/or their employer in terms of time and money. The results are not jeopardized if one facilitator has to leave or is temporarily not on form.

In a situation such as Sheila's, described above, a facilitator can find it difficult to pay full attention to the group if they have just been engaged in an intense confrontation with one individual. Allowing their co-facilitator to take primary responsibility for the next session can provide them with a valuable opportunity to distance themselves from the specific situation and refocus their attention on the whole group.

Use as a sounding board

A co-facilitator can also be used as a sounding board and check in analysing what is happening within the group and how best to respond to this in order to enable group members' learning. We have found that it is useful to make time at regular intervals throughout the work to reflect on events and consider any refinements or adjustments which you want to make to your co-facilitation. You have access to another professional viewpoint which can prompt you to re-examine your own. This is beneficial, even if you do not change your thinking, as the act of having to explain your view often forces you to consider the assumptions or evidence on which you have based it. What Heron (1989) refers to as the facilitator's skill of discrimination – being able to choose appropriate strategies – can be developed by having opportunities to discuss the reasoning for choices regarding interventions with a co-facilitator who can challenge your established thinking and contribute a different perspective on issues. One of the facilitators involved in our research commented on this aspect:

> 'Like many other facilitators, I have a model of facilitation that I hold dear… this can be a limiting factor if not challenged occasionally.'

Using your co-facilitator as a sounding board can be particularly helpful in uncovering some of your fundamental assumptions about facilitation. Even if you do not modify these as a result of your deliberations, it can help you to gain clarity about why you do what you do – thus increasing the purposefulness of your interventions.

Synergistic effect

This advantage builds on the one described above. When co-facilitators are working well together there is often a synergistic effect as the outcomes of their deliberations exceed their individual contributions. In co-facilitation, you are jointly engaged on working towards a shared goal in which you both have a vested interest and to which you are both committed. This means that, while you both understand the context in which your facilitative decisions are made, you have more than one mind considering the issues and difficulties you are addressing.

On many occasions when we have felt stuck and lacking in ideas to help advance a group or an individual, we have been able to develop a productive way forward as a direct result of bouncing our thinking around with our co-facilitator. Many of us find that our best ideas come from the exchange of views, thinking and concerns with others and co-facilitating has a very tangible benefit for us – and, in turn, for the groups we work with.

Choice of co-facilitator for particular interventions

When co-facilitating there is a choice of which facilitator is best placed to work with a particular group member or to intervene on a particular issue. This decision may be based on a variety of factors – the skills of the facilitator, the relationship which they have managed to develop with a group member, the gender of the facilitator or their theoretical background and approach (for example, whether Gestalt informs their facilitation style or whether they take a pyschodynamic approach). Since an individual's response to feedback is often influenced as much by the giver of the feedback as by the message itself, the ability to influence the likelihood of a positive reception is an important advantage of co-facilitating. This is particularly true when you need to challenge a group member's behaviour, for example, and anticipate that this might provoke a defensive reaction.

Increased capacity to work with complex issues

Another benefit of being able to divide the focus of attention between co-facilitators is the increased capacity to work with complex and challenging group issues. For example, a number of issues might arise simultaneously within the group and be best addressed by splitting into smaller groups or by one facilitator working with one participant while the co-facilitator continues to work with the rest of the group. Quite simply, having more than one facilitator creates more flexible options for working.

Although Heron (1989) does not refer to co-facilitation directly, he recognizes flexibility of style as the key to effective facilitation.

Changes of pace and style

We believe that each facilitator has an individual way of working with groups, even where they share fundamental assumptions about their work or have similar backgrounds. As such, by moving between co-facilitators in terms of who is leading or taking prime responsibility for a particular session, you can introduce variety of pace and style of delivery to enhance the overall effectiveness of the facilitation. By using such changes awarely, co-facilitators can ensure optimum levels of energy and interest are maintained among group members.

Differences in pace and style can also be used to ensure that a good match is obtained with the focus of the work at any particular point in time. For example, some facilitators have a very active style which can be used to generate energy within the group, while others might have a quiet, more reflective style which can help group members learn by taking a step back and contemplating an event. When working with a co-facilitator who has a highly active style, Joanna has modified her own approach to ensure that the group is also encouraged to reflect on their activity – thus ensuring that the overall facilitation style is well balanced to enable group members' learning.

Increased creativity

Co-facilitation can increase creativity in several ways. First, there is the synergistic effect already referred to. A co-facilitator is also a source of fresh ideas, different experiences, new techniques and activities which can supplement your own. However, there is also an important longer term benefit when the capacity for creative working increases as you continue working together, due to the exchanges about your professional practice. Co-facilitating is a really useful way of opening up your facilitation for professional review and comment. And as this can happen while you are engaged in the work itself, there is no need to make additional demands on your time. It also ensures the timeliness of any feedback exchanged, since this can be given immediately after the event or action being reviewed, which in turn is likely to enhance the quality of the feedback.

Our abilities as facilitators have benefited as a result of this type of professional exchange and we have certainly gained many new ideas. We have also felt supported by co-facilitators in taking particular risks with groups or in trying out new approaches, as the responsibility for the success of such initiatives is shared with another professional (as well as with group members).

This support is particularly important when facilitators are trying to work creatively, responding to the emerging needs of the group rather than using structured, off-the-shelf exercises. We have found that one of us typically produces the raw idea, which is then refined and developed in discussion with the other, therefore exposing the idea to testing as an intrinsic part of its development. As a result, we have a higher level of confidence in an untried idea than we would otherwise have and are therefore more inclined to be creative.

Accessing complementary skills

The group can benefit when more than one facilitator is working with them, if co-facilitators bring complementary skills, experiences, backgrounds and personalities to the work being undertaken. This has the effect of enriching the facilitation and the learning of group members. This effect often occurs, in our experience, when an external consultant co-facilitates with an internal trainer. Both have different qualities and experiences to offer to the group. For instance, the external consultant can provide a broad perspective of what is happening in other organizations and can be more objective about the issues which the group and business are facing than someone from the same company. The internal trainer can empathize with others from the same organization and offer insights regarding inside politics and how things get done most effectively. So, together, they can provide a more complete service to their client group.

Reducing the impact of facilitator limitations

We all have our own limitations or personal blocks as facilitators. A facilitator may be particularly inclined to notice or ignore certain intrapersonal or interpersonal issues, if they reflect their own concerns. In addition, if an issue arising within the group triggers an intense reaction in one facilitator they may be temporarily disabled in terms of their full ability to work with the group and it may be more appropriate for their co-facilitator to take prime responsibility for the session. A co-facilitator can also help guard against excessive attention being paid to certain issues by their partner, as they may be able to view the situation more objectively.

An example of this from our own experience is that some facilitators have a strong need to rescue others, which can limit their ability to challenge group members' behaviour or to let them experience challenging feedback from their colleagues. In this type of situation working with a co-facilitator can be useful, in that they are able to make the necessary challenge and also give feedback to the facilitator concerned to help them to break this limiting pattern.

Reduced dependency

The facilitator can often be a focus for group members' unresolved issues, particularly in relation to authority figures. With co-facilitation, the leadership or authority role is shared and thus this acts to reduce or dissipate the problem. Co-facilitators often model different leadership styles and behaviours, as they do in other areas too, and this provides group members with a variety of role models. It may be that one of these models will not trigger their unresolved issues and hence will allow the group member to start to develop a new relationship with those in authority positions.

Group members may put facilitators under pressure to conform to their own stereotypical expectations of those in authority roles, and co-facilitators can provide valuable support for each other in resisting the temptation of colluding with these expectations, where this would not be appropriate or useful for the group. Refusing to fall into these expected behaviours allows the opportunity for group members to find new ways of relating to those in authority and represents another way in which group members' dependency on the facilitators can be reduced.

Modelling appropriate behaviours

One of the most important ways in which co-facilitators can contribute added value to group members' learning is by modelling effective interpersonal behaviours in their own relationship. This is especially valuable if the focus of group members' development is interpersonal skills, because they have a live example of 'good practice' being enacted in front of them. Such modelling offers the group a distinctive advantage, as Corey and Corey (1992) have pointed out:

> 'what you model through what you do in the group is one of the most powerful ways of teaching members how to relate to one another constructively.'

It is simply not possible to offer group members this particular advantage if facilitating alone (other than by your handling of relationships with group members themselves, but this lacks the same consistency of effect). Demonstrating that differences of opinion can be productive when handled constructively can be an important issue for co-facilitators to model, since many organizations interpret disagreement as problematic and act to reduce or deny difference and diversity. For example, when working together with a group, we feel able to disagree with each other where we hold different views – while still maintaining our individual credibility by showing that we find such disagreement acceptable and a source of creative tension. Other forms of modelling, such as that involved in male–female co-facilitating, can also be important as a source of learning if appropriate, independent and mutually supportive roles are demonstrated. This particular benefit of co-facilitating was considered very valuable by facilitators involved in our research, as the following comments show:

> 'They saw us trusting each other and respecting each other, and it helped them see how they could be different... It also helped them to experiment with expressing feeling as they saw us being open with each other.'

> 'There was some evidence that we had provided a useful role model as I saw some of our behaviours usefully incorporated into group behaviour.'

This benefit of co-facilitation will be explored in greater depth in Chapter 8 when we examine the impact of co-facilitation on the group.

Facilitator development

Co-facilitating offers both (all) partners support and practical help in their continuing professional development. Some group members may not be sufficiently skilled in giving feedback, especially of a challenging or intensive kind, to be able to provide meaningful feedback for facilitators on their level of competence. For example, sometimes their interpretation of facilitator skill may depend on their level of enjoyment rather than the learning gained – which may not become apparent until a later date. In addition, the process of engaging in some in-depth development work may be difficult and at times painful for the individual and it is often only in hindsight, in our experience, that they recognize the value of the facilitator's work.

When facilitators work together, one of the major benefits is the provision of a source of skilled feedback from someone who appreciates the objectives, the intended methods of achieving these, the difficulties, the context and the resulting requirements from the facilitators. A co-facilitator can provide direct feedback from someone who has been present at the events under review, rather than someone who heard about what happened through the filtering of the facilitator's own perception. This professional feedback can greatly enhance a facilitator's development, both in the short term and over longer periods of time. It can also help ensure that you maintain an accurate image of your ability as a facilitator, rather than becoming overly reliant upon feedback from group members which might encourage some facilitators to seek their good opinion rather than focus on maximizing their learning.

This important benefit of co-facilitating will be explored in more depth in Chapter 5, when we explore ways in which the relationship between co-facilitators can be developed.

Facilitator support

Good facilitation often requires the facilitator to work with a minimal or no script, as they respond to the particular needs of the group with which they are working. This approach places significant demands on the facilitator, which Berry (1993) has identified: 'Facilitating in the unknown brings facilitators immediately to their own "growing edge". This is both exciting and terrifying.' Co-facilitating is one effective way of getting support in such testing situations, from someone who understands the stresses and demands of the facilitator's role. It may also be that your 'growing edge' is different from that of your co-facilitator, so that you can each offer guidance and practical as well as emotional support in different areas as appropriate.

REFLECTION

▶ When reflecting on your own experiences of co-facilitating, how well do you think you have been able to capitalize on these potential benefits?

▶ Have you been able to identify any other advantages, based on your co-facilitative experience?

▶ Have you worked better with some co-facilitators than with others? If so, what do you believe has made the difference?

▶ Have you found particular benefits especially easy or difficult to achieve? Why do you think this is?

▶ How do you think you could improve your co-facilitative practice as a result of this reflection? Is there any action you can start to take?

Advantages: conclusions

There are many important advantages to be gained from co-facilitating, both for the facilitators themselves and for the groups with which they work. Later chapters in this book explore how these benefits can best be captured, by examining ways in which the relationship between co-facilitators can be developed. Certainly the facilitators with whom we conducted our research were aware that the realization of these potential advantages was dependent on the quality of the relationship established between co-facilitators, thereby highlighting the importance of developing good working relationships. Two representative comments were:

'Maybe if we focused on this question [ie, the potential benefits] more often, we might attach more importance to the relationship with our co-facilitators.'

'The quality of the relationship between co-facilitators underlies everything, it is a determinant of what happens in the group and vice versa.'

It is certainly our strong belief, based on our own experiences as co-facilitators, that the quality of the relationship between co-facilitators is critical in determining their level of working effectiveness.

THE DISADVANTAGES OF CO-FACILITATING

Some of the literature on facilitation briefly explores the disadvantages of co-facilitating, to set against the possible advantages. Again, these are potential difficulties and it is our belief, based on our own experiences as co-facilitators and on our research findings, that disadvantages can be avoided or minimized *providing* that co-facilitators are willing and able to explore their own working relationship and its level of effectiveness. We would further suggest that the process of working through such difficulties is often positive and developmental for the co-facilitators involved and, therefore, ultimately for the groups with which they work.

The group's perception

Spinks and Clements (1993) have identified several adverse responses that groups may have to co-facilitators, based on assumptions that:

- the group must be perceived as difficult and requiring additional resources;
- one facilitator must be a learner;
- it is a waste of expensive resources.

We, too, have found that this can occasionally be the case, although we must emphasize that in many situations working with more than one facilitator is not seen by groups or their organizational sponsors as being in any way problematic or wasteful. Where a problem of perception does exist, however, we have found that it can be easily managed by being open with group members about the rationale for there being more than one facilitator and by highlighting the potential benefits. Ultimately, of course, the most effective argument is the quality of the work carried out by the co-facilitators, which speaks for itself.

Unequal distribution of work

When co-facilitating, there can be a tendency for one facilitator to rely on their partner to make all the challenging interventions on individual or group issues. This results in an unequal distribution of the more demanding work, which can leave one facilitator under-stretched while their colleague is under considerably more personal and professional pressure. Occasionally, such inequality may be appropriate, depending on the personal circumstances or abilities of both co-facilitators. However, if a continuing imbalance is not the result of a conscious decision by both parties, the informal working contract operating between the co-facilitators needs to be addressed. This type of behaviour pattern can also lead to co-facilitators being labelled, for example, as the 'hard' or 'soft' one, which may encourage group members' tendencies to view people in a one-dimensional or stereotypical way.

Conflicting messages

One major disadvantage can occur when co-facilitators have fundamentally different approaches to their work, since such significant differences can result in them working at cross-purposes. As one facilitator commented: 'where the difference is so wide it seems to negate both styles.' While this can have a detrimental effect on the co-facilitators themselves, in that neither is able to progress the work in the way that they see as being most effective and therefore their impact may be reduced, it also results in group members receiving conflicting messages about which attitudes and behaviours are valued and appropriate within the group. They are then left feeling confused and insecure, and these emotions might in turn inhibit their learning or their ability to make business decisions.

Conflicting co-facilitator styles can also result in factions or cliques forming among group members, as they align themselves with a particular facilitator. This can lead to interventions from a less favoured facilitator being ignored or given less attention, which can also have a negative impact on group members' learning.

We have noted this difficulty on several occasions when we have been group members. Co-facilitators have clearly held different models of personal and professional effectiveness and, rather than these being presented as options from which group members can choose or to which they can add, factions have formed within the group according to which model of facilitation they prefer. Difference, rather than being perceived

23

as a source of added value, has been interpreted as a source of competition between the co-facilitators, which has impacted negatively on group members' learning.

In Chapter 3 we provide practical advice on how to establish effective working relationships with your co-facilitators, which we hope will help you to avoid major problems. Having a good understanding of the values and beliefs that inform your own approach to facilitation, and that of your co-facilitator, will certainly help you to avoid potential pitfalls, or at least to recognize those which may be most relevant to you both in your work together.

Alternatively, if you find yourself experiencing difficulty in working well with a co-facilitator, Chapter 6 suggests a number of ways to address the problems between you. It is important that you do not let your differences become unproductive, in terms of communicating conflicting and confusing messages to group members, as this is likely to impact adversely on their learning in the ways described above.

Competition

Differences such as these can result in co-facilitators becoming competitive with each other. They may then engage in behaviours, either consciously or unconsciously, designed to promote their own popularity rather than group members' learning. Group members can exacerbate this situation, by playing off one facilitator against another – rather like children sometimes do with their parents!

We can remember instances when we have found ourselves in competition with co-facilitators. Often the competition has emerged indirectly and unconsciously (at the time) in subtle comments or behaviours, such as one facilitator constantly offering a more comprehensive explanation of an activity when their partner has already introduced it adequately. This can subtly undermine the credibility of the other co-facilitator. Unless this type of behaviour is identified and then discussed it will continue to limit the effectiveness of both facilitators.

Adverse modelling

When the relationship between co-facilitators is competitive, closed or mistrusting, negative modelling of interpersonal behaviours can occur. This is especially destructive when the co-facilitators involved are not able or willing to acknowledge and work through these issues, either by themselves or with group members. Ineffective behaviour in dealing with interpersonal difficulties is then modelled, and may reinforce group members in existing patterns of their own rather than supporting their development.

This situation can also occur when male–female co-facilitators work together, if they replicate stereotypical and limiting behaviours. An example would be when the male facilitator makes all the challenging interventions, leaving his female partner to provide solace and comfort to group members. While both functions can be useful, being unconsciously stuck in such a fixed pattern of behaviour is not helpful in enabling group members' own learning.

Over-facilitation

If co-facilitators are inclined to be active in terms of the number of interventions they typically make, group members may not be allowed the time and space in which to develop their own capacity to make appropriate interventions. This can seriously limit the development opportunities for individual group members. Co-facilitators need to ensure that their facilitation does not become overwhelming and limit, rather than enhance, their effectiveness.

This type of co-facilitator behaviour can also be an outcome of competition arising between the facilitators, where they are constantly trying to outdo each other in terms of the quality and/or quantity of their interventions.

Different response times

Co-facilitators may have different response times, in that one has a tendency to intervene very quickly in response to an event within the group while another tends to wait in order to allow opportunity for the group members to make an appropriate intervention. In this situation, one facilitator may be seen as doing all the work or, conversely, as being overly obtrusive. It can be very frustrating for a co-facilitator who allows space to find that this is constantly taken, not by participants, but by their partner! Co-facilitators need to identify how they will ensure that they both have opportunities to contribute to group members' learning, so that the benefits of having more than one facilitator are not lost.

Reinforcement of limitations

If co-facilitators share the same limitations, then they may reinforce these in each other rather than challenging them. For example, if co-facilitators do not like confronting issues or lack the skills to do this effectively, they may rationalize this as not forming an appropriate part of their role and, by their collusion, reinforce this limitation in their facilitation.

Extra demands on energy

When acting as a co-facilitator, you need to pay attention not only to the group and its individual members, but also to your co-facilitator and the relationship between the two of you. Especially when there are some difficulties associated with the relationship, it may take considerable extra resources of energy to attend adequately to these. If the potential advantages of working together are not being realized, you may feel disinclined to expend this energy.

We have sometimes experienced this situation when working with an inexperienced trainer, who is hoping to develop their skills by working alongside someone more experienced. It can be demanding to be paying attention to your co-facilitator as well as to the group and what you are trying to achieve, particularly when the work is highly challenging. Conversely, when we have worked together, we have not expended this additional energy as we are familiar and confident with each other's facilitation style and level of competence.

REFLECTION

▶ To what extent have you been able to avoid these potential disadvantages in your own co-facilitation practice?

▶ Have you experienced any other disadvantages?

▶ Have you found it difficult to avoid any particular disadvantages? Why do you think this is?

▶ Have you experienced more of these disadvantages with particular facilitators? If so, why do you think this is?

▶ Using your reflections, what recommendations would you make to improve your co-facilitative practice? Are there any actions you could take?

Disadvantages: conclusions

Their examination of some of the difficulties of co-facilitating led Spinks and Clements (1993) to conclude that you should not co-facilitate, in the way in which we understand this. Instead, they recommend that one facilitator acts as scribe, recording decisions made by the group, while the other facilitator takes responsibility for leading the group-work. This seems to us to be an overreaction to the potential problems identified, treating them as insoluble, and ignores the many potential advantages which can be gained from co-facilitation.

We believe that a more constructive approach is to explore ways in which co-facilitators can recognize the issues involved and work to address them where they exist. Our own experience, supported by our research, demonstrates that the process of dealing with any difficulties experienced can, of itself, be developmental for the individuals concerned and for their professional practice.

SUMMARY

After reading this chapter, you should have a clear understanding of the essential characteristics and the purpose of both facilitation and co-facilitation, since this is the foundation stone on which the book is built. We have identified and explored the potential advantages and disadvantages of co-facilitation in some depth, to encourage you to reflect on your own experience as a co-facilitator and to identify to what degree you have been able to benefit from its advantages and avoid some of its worst disadvantages. We believe, based not only on our own experience but also on that of other experienced and able facilitators involved in our research, that the potential advantages of co-facilitation far outweigh the possible disadvantages – both for the co-facilitators themselves and for the groups with whom they work.

As you read on through the rest of this book you will find out how you can capitalize on the potential advantages of co-facilitating and avoid some of the disadvantages. The key to this lies in paying good attention to your relationship with your co-facilitators. There is plenty of practical help provided in the following chapters to enable you to do this.

For those who have not yet worked as a co-facilitator, we hope that our identification of the benefits has provided you with a clear sense of what you can gain, and that this will encourage you to try out the role and extend your professional practice.

3

The Dynamics of Working with a Co-facilitator

In the co-facilitative relationship (as in any relationship) there are two ongoing levels of communication. This is often referred to in other studies of human relating by such phrases as 'content and process', 'words and music', the 'light and shadow', among many other labels. All of these refer to the fact that there is an open level of communicating, which is easily seen, understood and which tends to be within our awareness. They also refer to a 'hidden' or 'inner' level of communication, which can often be outside our immediate awareness.

Where the content level of working is concerned with the 'what', the process level deals with the 'how'. The content level is often obvious and easily identified, while the process level is often hidden from immediate awareness. We have found that many facilitators focus their attention on the content elements of working, at the cost of them paying attention to the process.

In our research, we found that most of the difficulties faced by co-facilitators emerged from a process that had not been dealt with effectively. When the process is not addressed, it will impact on the work at a content level. For example, co-facilitators who have unresolved issues in their relationship will be less effective in supporting each other in their work with a group. This also causes organizing an event to be dealt with less effectively. The process between them has therefore impacted on their relationship, and in turn on the practical aspects of the work. The content and process are inextricably linked, and each will impact on the other. The process is more difficult to deal with, but is much more powerful in its effect. Both of these levels are important enough to affect the success of your co-facilitation practice. Both need to be addressed, as both contribute to excellence in co-facilitative practice.

In this book, we refer to the content level of communication as the 'outer' elements of co-facilitation because it is immediately obvious, while the process level of communication is referred to as the 'inner' elements of the co-facilitative relationship because of its less immediately obvious nature.

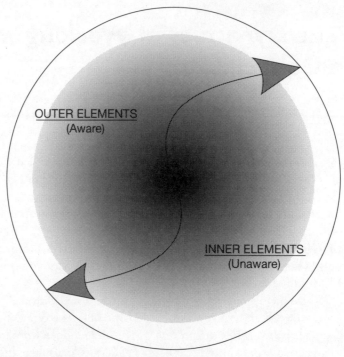

Figure 3.1   The whole co-facilitative relationship

THE OUTER ELEMENTS OF THE CO-FACILITATIVE RELATIONSHIP

Within any co-facilitative relationship, there are a number of dynamics which are practical and within the immediate awareness of the facilitators. As these issues are usually within awareness, and at a surface level, we have labelled them the 'outer' elements of the co-facilitative relationship. These tend to be the issues that many co-facilitators address first, but they also need to be continually considered throughout the practice.

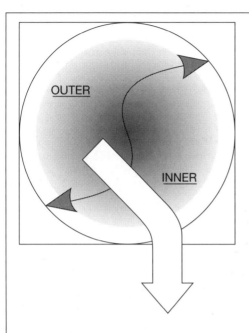

Characteristics

- Usually within awareness
- Commonly addressed by one or both facilitators
- Visible surface of the relationship, noticeable by outside parties

Common elements

- Shared aims/objectives for the work
- Shared approach to learning
- Practical agreement on the work arrangements
- Sharing of views and analysis of issues
- Diagnosing the work jointly
- Clear co-facilitative contracting
- Regular reviews
- Joint ownership/responsibility
- Agreed groundrules
- Support
- Interest in making co-facilitation successful

Figure 3.2   The 'outer' elements of the co-facilitative relationship

This chapter examines the 'what' of how co-facilitators can work together. These are issues around designing, arranging, coordinating and planning the work together, and which the facilitators tend to work openly with. The 'inner' elements (discussed in the following chapter) and 'outer' elements (discussed here) of co-facilitation are equally important.

There are a number of elements within this outer aspect of co-facilitation. The following are some of those which we have found most commonly in co-facilitative relationships. You will be able to add to these according to your own experiences.

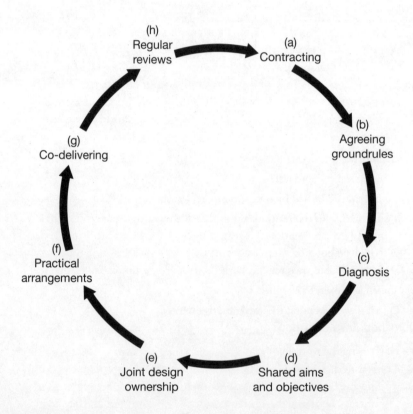

Figure 3.3   A cycle for the practical elements in co-facilitation

(a) Contracting

Contracting is a key part of working with a co-facilitator. It is often talked about, but in our experience, we find it is rarely done very well, nor is it maintained or reviewed throughout the work together. Ideally some form of contracting should happen with all people involved in this work, the client(s), the group(s) and the co-facilitator.

The contract may be for a specific piece of work or it may be for a longer period of time. Whichever of these it is, you will need to revisit and review the contract between you on a regular basis.

What is a contract?

One of the problems with contracting is that it sounds very formal and structured. For this reason it often puts facilitators off carrying it out unless absolutely necessary. The word 'contract' is a piece of jargon in this context, but put simply, a contract is *an agreement between you*. For facilitators, it is about how you want to work together. In the excitement and urgency of a piece of facilitation, the preparation for the work often means that this agreement is forgotten and often not reviewed.

Why should we contract?

Contracting is the chance to examine any issues or differences between your ways of working, before they arise as a problem. It is far better to do it this way than try and manage any difficulties at the time of running a group together. Contracting also allows you to consider the work you are about to carry out, and therefore to examine your practice and generally the way you work. It is therefore a potentially powerful learning tool for you to utilize.

When should we contract?

Contracts are not a 'one-off' event; they need to be discussed initially, re-visited, reviewed during the work and after the work is completed. The initial discussion needs to include some agreement regarding the contract between the co-facilitators. The contractual discussion should include points relating to the work itself, eg the training event. It should also include discussion between the co-facilitators about the relationship between them. We suggest that this is reviewed at regular intervals during the work, but this process needs to be more defined than the original discussion, and this should happen before the co-facilitation itself is carried out.

CHECKLIST OF QUESTIONS FOR THE CO-FACILITATIVE CONTRACT

- [ ] What exactly is the work we are doing?
- [ ] What are we aiming to achieve?
- [ ] Who is doing what?
- [ ] What is my role in this?
- [ ] What is your role in this?
- [ ] Who (if anyone) is liaising with the client?
- [ ] Who (if anyone) is leading the facilitation?
- [ ] How will we review the work and our work as co-facilitators?
- [ ] What are our groundrules for working together? (Be specific)
- [ ] What feedback, support and challenge do I want from my co-facilitator?
- [ ] What am I not willing to do/accept?
- [ ] What happens if one of us breaks our contract?
- [ ] What decisions can/cannot be made in the absence of each facilitator?
- [ ] How will we learn from each other?

What should the contract include?

It can include many aspects of the work, some of which are in the checklist opposite.

For those facilitators who would normally contract with a client, consider the benefits that the client contracting gives. How might you transfer these benefits to your co-facilitative relationship?

The checklist contains some questions that you might like to consider before drawing up a contract with your co-facilitator:

(b) Agreeing groundrules

One part of contracting is setting what are often referred to as 'groundrules'. Trainers and facilitators often set groundrules for teams and groups. This is also a useful and necessary procedure in co-facilitative practice.

Even thinking about your answer to the question about what is acceptable and unacceptable to you, will aid the process and the work between you and your co-facilitator.

This obviously links very closely to the contracting mentioned above, but the elements of the groundrules are usually drawn from experience, and are often decided upon throughout the work together. Where the contracting tends to be based upon the formal aspects of the work such as the roles each of you will take, the groundrules tend to focus on behavioural aspects between you. The range of areas to agree on are endless, but in our experience some common areas for discussion between co-facilitators are:

- What is it OK or not to discuss in front of the group?
- Is it OK to disagree in front of the group?
- Are we allowed to interrupt each other?
- Can I change my session content according to how it is going?
- Am I allowed to go over time/finish early in my sessions?
- How and when will we review?
- What feedback do I want and how would I like it given and when?
- What are we not going to do in the way we facilitate?

A good way of testing your groundrules is to imagine that they are the groundrules *you* are being asked to adhere to. Are they groundrules that you could work with, in terms of type, quality and quantity?

The groundrules that we like to have are often a reflection of ourselves and the type of co-facilitative relationship that we have. In this sense they can be used in your own personal development. We recently came across a facilitator who insisted that their co-facilitator never interrupted them at all and never commented during any session that they were leading. In reviewing this it became clear that they did not have any understanding of their co-facilitator's approaches and skills, resulting in a lack of trust between them. What do your groundrules indicate about you?

(c) Diagnosis of the work

Within the early stages of the work, you will be considering how to carry out the diagnosis of the work group/client that you are doing the work for.

As co-facilitators, one advantage of working in a pair is that you are likely to be able to get two views and opinions on the diagnosis of the work. The negative side to this is that unless you establish a joint understanding of the situation, then you are going to be working to separate and different objectives. Joint diagnosis is therefore a key element to successful co-facilitation. At the very least the diagnosis needs to be agreed with your co-facilitator and ideally it should be carried out together.

There are a number of questions that you might use as a start to this joint diagnosis. These include the following.

Who is the target group/client?

A common difference here is when one facilitator considers the group to be the target client, when the other considers the initial instigator of the work (such as a department head) to be the client. It may be that either or both are correct, the key being that it has been discussed and agreed between co-facilitators.

What is the context?

There will have been, and still will be, many issues not directly related to the work, but in the context of the work. The relevance of these can be easily missed, and yet they can have a major impact on the work. Some of these are factual issues, such as how long the group has been together, and some other issues may be less immediately obvious, such as the culture within which the group operates. They will all have an influence on the work. The following are a few examples of the types of contextual issues you might consider the work of the group itself, the last programme/training event they were on, how they are managed/led, whether they have been told to attend or whether they have chosen to, the performance of the company, the working environment, the type of work itself, etc. Each co-facilitator will place relevance and importance on different contextual issues. Discussion of these will add greatly to the work you carry out as co-facilitators.

What do we already know?

Between you and your co-facilitator, you will find that you already know quite a lot about the work. As co-facilitators you will have noticed different things within the client group, as well as getting the 'official' information on the work.

Who will diagnose?

Options for your diagnosis of the work are doubled when you work with a co-facilitator. Your options are to carry the diagnosis out as a pair or one individual may carry it out for the pairing. As a pair you are likely to get a fuller diagnosis of the situation, based on the richness which can be gathered from two views. However, this needs to be balanced against the cost in time of having two of you do this.

There are also some relationship issues to be considered in this part of the work. Whenever you meet a client group, you are establishing and developing the relationship, therefore if one facilitator carries out the diagnosis alone, what is the likely effect on the relationship of the group with both facilitators? This is of course a consideration throughout any contact with clients, but it is at this early stage that the type of relationship is established for the future work together. Conscious and subconscious decisions are taken by individuals within groups about facilitators. We find these often to be around credibility, power, the relationship between the facilitators, seniority and influence, among many others.

The issue within this question of who carries out the diagnosis, therefore, needs to be considered while bearing in mind that not only are you collecting data, but you are also establishing a relationship which will affect any future work carried out. One way you might like to consider this is in terms of relationship management. If you think of your relationship with the client and group as an element to be managed, what do you need to do to establish and maintain a good relationship for both co-facilitators?

What methods should we use?

Each of you will have your favourite and preferred methods to diagnose the work. With two facilitators, you have the opportunity to learn other new methods and approaches. The key element in terms of your relationship is to be able to pick the most appropriate method for the particular piece of work. There are obviously a number of methods including individual interview, group meetings to identify need and questionnaires. It is not our aim here to go through the methods you might use to diagnose the client needs, but for each method you will need to discuss the impact on your co-facilitative practice and the relationship for each of you with the client. For example, you will need to discuss who carries out the interview, how you pass the information to your co-facilitator and how you use less formal insights such as your intuitive sense or feelings towards the client?

Within the diagnosis the above are some of the main questions in reference to your co-facilitative practice. The following questions could also be discussed with your co-facilitator:

- What will we do with the data and how will we present it back to the client?
- Do we need to diagnose?
- What is the client's diagnosis?

(d) Shared aims and objectives

An obvious but often overlooked area of working together is to share and understand the objectives for the work. These objectives fall into different categories as follows.

Overall purpose

The work will have an overall purpose, so this purpose needs to be discussed with your co-facilitator. We have found that this seemingly simple and obvious point, when it is unresolved, is often at the root of later problems.

Desired outcomes

The first broad objective is the desired outcome for the group and individuals within it. If it is an organizational programme, then what are the objectives for the organization, group and individuals linked to the work? If these are stated as desired outcomes, it will help focus your work.

Facilitator outcomes

Secondly, what are the objectives for each of the facilitators? What does each facilitator want from this event? This area is often glanced over until the objectives of one or both facilitators are not being met. You will both have outcomes for yourself that you are aiming for. These are more likely to be achieved if they are explicit and shared with your co-facilitator.

Core objectives

Within each of the two sets of outcomes, there will be a *key* outcome that you are attempting to facilitate. If you could strip away all the other objectives, what is left at the core? In other words, what is the one objective that must happen?

Often it will seem that there are too many outcomes that you are attempting to achieve. In this case you will need to be clear about the core objectives required against those desired. This in itself, done jointly with your co-facilitator, will enhance your co-facilitative practice. The search for purpose is an imperative and essential one.

During the period over which the work is carried out, the work objectives may change or alter. This is why objectives and contracts need to be regularly reviewed and amended, as often the objectives at the start of the work may be different from those near the end of the work.

Measures

Finally, how will you know if you have achieved your objectives? It is likely that you have some kind of idea about what a successful outcome means. This needs to be made explicit. If you can identify indicators and measures, you have a greater chance of achieving them.

(e) Joint design ownership

Shared ownership from both facilitators will produce greater understanding and commitment towards the work. Many of the co-facilitators with whom we have worked have reported joint ownership as a key contributory factor in either the success or failure of their co-facilitative work. Ownership for the work can be gained or lost at any stage along the course of the work. It is easy to lose joint ownership, for example, if one facilitator has all the client contact, the co-facilitator may feel detached from the work. Having a co-facilitator poses a particular issue in this context, as it may be easier to get one facilitator owning the work. However, we have found that joint ownership tends to produce higher levels of satisfaction with the work.

Shared design ownership

Apart from the diagnosis work discussed above, joint ownership is often achieved at the design stage of the work. There are a number of models for carrying out the design (for a fuller understanding of these models read Chapter 7). Options include:

1 joint designing;
2 one facilitator designing and then discussing alterations with the co-facilitator;
3 one facilitator taking responsibility for the whole design.

The following continuum displays these choices:

1	2	3
1. Joint design responsibility	2. One designs and then discuss	3. Single responsibility for design

These are only three points on the continuum. You can choose a position at any point between these options. Any of these can work for you as co-facilitators. Each choice will also have implications for the relationship between co-facilitators and for ownership of the work.

One facilitator designing or one facilitator designing and then discussing the design, is often the easiest and quickest method. For both facilitators to feel comfortable with this takes a high level of understanding, so it often works better with co-facilitators who are used to working together. It can also work well when one facilitator is more experienced or knowledgeable than the other.

ACTIVITY: DESIGN PREPARATION

Interview your co-facilitator using the following questions. (Use these questions in an order that makes sense for you.)

Question	Facilitator 1	Facilitator 2
What are your preferences for how to design?		
Who is designing?		
When?		
What parts are we each designing?		
What theoretical models or approaches do you want to use for this piece of work?		
How would you describe your approach to facilitation?		
What do you want to get out of this piece of work?		
What do you want from me?		
What are your hopes and concerns about co-designing?		

In our experience, joint design is one of the most difficult and yet most effective ways of working as co-facilitators. The relationship needs to have a good level of interpersonal skills, assertion, negotiating and the ability to deal with differences.

There are many considerations to be addressed during the design including methods for designs, basic design assumptions, levels of knowledge, approaches to the work, flexibility in the design and how to design in a way which meets both co-facilitators' needs.

Before carrying out the design, try the design preparation activity with your co-facilitator.

(f) Practical arrangements and who does what (roles)

As co-facilitators you will need to decide who organizes any work that you are carrying out. You might like to write down your own checklist, but opposite there are a few questions to consider with your co-facilitator.

(g) Co-delivering the work

There are obvious decisions to be made with your co-facilitator about how you will work during the actual facilitation/training. This is the point at which the preparation work is over, and all the planning and preparation is put into practice.

There are a number of areas for you to consider in this stage of the work. All the prior preparation so far discussed is of course still relevant and important. Chapter 7 outlines some possible ways of working together and within this co-facilitators need to agree how the work is done (methods). What is each facilitator's preference regarding working methods? For example, your co-facilitator may like to use an approach which relies heavily on presentation and theoretical input. How would this be matched with a co-facilitator who prefers an approach which relies heavily on process observation and non-theory based training? The micro skills of training and facilitation are also a consideration. For example, even if you agree to use an exercise and review method of training, what type of exercise and how to review are still considerations which need to be agreed.

You need to have in mind your own preferred methods of working. In the same light, you will need to find a way of matching your ideas for how people learn and how this can be facilitated. One way of doing this is to look at values and beliefs (see Chapter 4). Successful work in this

CHECKLIST FOR ARRANGING THE CO-FACILITATION

☐ Who is booking and agreeing the dates?

☐ Who designs, and how?

☐ Who leads what sessions?

☐ Who prepares, and how?

☐ Where will the work be, and who is arranging this?

☐ Who is the client link?

☐ What are the arrangements regarding payment/fees, and cancellation costs?

☐ Who is liaising with the venue?

☐ What do we need at the venue (such as room layout etc)?

☐ Who arranges the written work/handouts/equipment etc?

☐ Who is carrying out the administration for delegates (such as joining instructions)?

☐ What are our roles within the work itself?

(See examples of different types of relationships in Chapter 7.)

area relies heavily on co-facilitators' willingness to try new ways and an openness to different ways of working.

(h) Regular reviews/sharing of views and interpretations

Development of your co-facilitative practice can happen in many ways. One of the key methods for this is review of both the work and your co-facilitative practice. We find that reviews are rarely done well, ironically, especially if the work is perceived to be going well. How often do excellent reviews take place only because something has not gone well? Reviewing actually offers much more of an opportunity than only exploring something that has not worked as well as hoped. It promotes learning, is a chance for feedback and is a support mechanism, as well as improving future work done.

What to review

Each facilitator will have their preferred methods for reviewing. As you progress in your co-facilitative relationship, you will develop the methods which suit you and work best for you. Here is one structure you could try for your reviewing.

1   Reviewing the work:
   ● What happened (factually)?
   ● What are your opinions/interpretations of what happened?
   ● How do you feel about the work?
   ● What else needs to be done/not done next time?

2   Reviewing the group and individuals within it:
   ● What have you noticed generally about the group and individuals?
   ● How would you describe the group process?
   ● What do you notice about the individuals in the group?
   ● How do you feel about the group and individuals?
   ● Who are the key individuals within the group.
   ● What is the best way of facilitating the group and individuals within it?
   ● What will you do differently next time?

3   Feedback to each other:
   ● What did you notice?

- What are your views and interpretations about what you noticed?
- How did you respond to that?
- What suggestions do you you have for your co-facilitators as to what they could do more or less of next time?

4   Reviewing the co-facilitation:
- Is the co-facilitation matching the agreed contract?
- Does the contract need changing or adding to?
- How can you improve your co-facilitative practice?
- What will you do differently next time?

How to review

Your groundrules and contracting between you should include something about how to review. The key element is to ensure that you do review in some form. Here are some considerations for how to do this (as opposed to the 'what' discussed above).

- Are you going to have a time limit for each facilitator to review?
- Are you going to have a structure to your reviewing or have a free flow of discussion?
- Is the discussion going to include feedback and, if it does, what feedback are you going to include?
- What constitutes good reviewing for you?

SUMMARY

In your co-facilitative practice there are two broad areas of focus – the 'inner' and the 'outer' levels of co-facilitation. This chapter outlines the outer level of co-facilitation. Within this outer level are the elements which are usually in the awareness of co-facilitation, this is the content level of communication between co-facilitators. The chapter outlines a cycle and how the outer level of co-facilitation relates to this cycle. The elements in this cycle are as follows.

(a) *Contracting.* Agreeing both the formal and informal aspects of how co-facilitators will work together.

(b) *Agreeing groundrules.* Understanding and agreeing the informal aspects of how each facilitator wants to work.

(c) *Diagnosis.* Finding a way of jointly diagnosing that allows ownership by both facilitators.

(d) *Shared aims and objectives.* Defining and agreeing the desired and core outcomes for the work, and for each facilitator.

(e) *Joint design ownership.* Co-designing to ensure that the design incorporates the best approaches of each facilitator and ensuring ownership by both facilitators.

(f) *Practical arrangements.* Organizing the work and deciding roles.

(g) *Co-delivering.* Matching and utilizing the skills of each facilitator, and using the advantages of having two facilitators.

(h) *Regular reviews* the work and the co-facilitation, during and after the work is done.

This chapter takes the practising co-facilitator through practical steps in developing their co-facilitation. The following chapter examines the 'inner' level of co-facilitation – the process dynamics that are present in the relationship between co-facilitators. These dynamics, as you will see, are less immediately obvious than the elements mentioned in this chapter, but are equally if not more important.

4

The Inner Dynamics of the Co-facilitative Relationship

Have you ever worked with someone and found that although both of you are technically fully competent, for some reason you just do not seem to be effective together? All the work itself may have been fine, but still the relationship between you just fails to be fully effective. What is going on here? Both of you carry out all the 'outer' elements, practical arrangements and organizing discussed in the previous chapter, but still the pairing is not as good as you know it could be.

Alternatively, have you ever worked with someone where everything between you simply clicks? You seem to have a natural rapport, you seem to instinctively be working well together and you know how best to work as a pair. The partnership just seems to thrive without trying and you look forward to working with them. What is going on here? How do you explain this?

In relation to co-facilitation, the previous chapter explores some of the issues around the content level of working, the planning, organizing, coordinating etc, and the elements that you can work on to improve your co-facilitating practice.

In this chapter we will be looking at the hidden or process level. There are many possible process dynamics going on at any one time. This chapter will outline the most common process dynamics that occur between co-facilitators. It will take you on a journey through each of these dynamics, and allow you to reflect on your own practice and experience.

The following model is a summary of the inner parts of the relationship between co-facilitators.

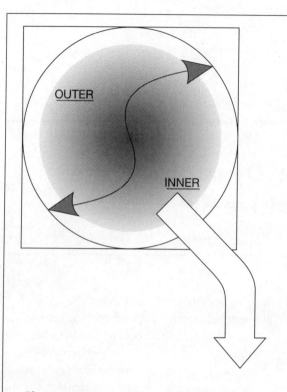

Characteristics

- Usually out of awareness
- Deeply held patterns of behaviour
- Foundations of the behaviours shown in outer elements
- Hidden parts of the relationship not immediately visible to outside parties

Common elements

- Power positions
- Quality of contact
- Projection
- Transference
- Core values
- Needs
- Differences and similarities

Figure 4.1   The inner elements of the co-facilitative relationship

---

REFLECTION

▶   Think of one of your experiences of co-facilitation.
    What comes to mind and what is the most significant
    thing about this relationship?
▶   Write down some key words which come to mind to
    describe the relationship.
▶   Now take a look at the set of words that you have
    written down. What can you conclude or learn from
    this?

The frameworks available to evaluate and make sense of your co-facilitative practice are many and varied. In fact, any process model may shed light on your experiences. We would strongly encourage you to use your own favourite models in your search for co-facilitative excellence. We shared many of our models to analyse co-facilitative practice. In fact one of the major benefits of working with someone else is the richness that can be found in sharing, working with, using and critically evaluating each other's models and approaches. Use the following as another model to add to your own.

POWER POSITIONS

When you work with another facilitator, how do you see yourself in relation to them? Is it by amount of expertise? Is it level of knowledge? Is it ability to influence? Is it popularity with a group? Or is it by some other measure?

When co-facilitators work together, each of them will use their own measures for seeing themselves in relation to the other. Type of measures will vary greatly, and each of us will have our own favourites. In some ways the type of measures are not important. What is important is the process that each of us go through in doing this. In what ways do we put ourselves in a one-up or one-down position in relation to our co-facilitator? It is these one-up or one-down positions that we have labelled the first dynamic we are going to work through – *power positions*.

One-down.

Our definition of this dynamic is when:

> a facilitator perceives themselves as being in a 'lower' position to their co-facilitator, using whatever criteria they choose. They then act in a way that reinforces this view of themselves.

Being one-down may not be necessarily just verbally putting yourself down in relation to the other facilitator (although this is often a clue that this dynamic is happening). There are many different responses to being in a one-down position. It may involve introjection (swallowing down whole what you are told without evaluating it for yourself). It may involve an internal message being played about your worth, for example, telling yourself that you are not very skilled, resulting in a lack of confidence. It often involves feeling persecuted or being in a 'victim' role. We have heard facilitators often introduce themselves to a group as 'Here to learn from…', when the actual agreement between facilitators was equality. Again the above examples relate to unawareness of being one-down.

There are many ways in which co-facilitators put themselves in a one-down position. However, there are some common patterns of behaviour that we have seen repeatedly across our work with facilitators. The following examples are some of the most common ways in which a facilitator can put themselves in a one-down position. The examples we have outlined here are:

- Victim
- 'I know nothing'
- 'I'm just here to learn'.

Victim

The Drama Triangle put forward by Karpman (1971) provides a useful framework for exploring some of these positions. It states that on a process level we can get into three patterns of behaviours or roles:

1. Persecutor (one-up position)
2. Rescuer (one-up position)
3. Victim (one-down position).

This Drama Triangle is shown in Figure 4.2.

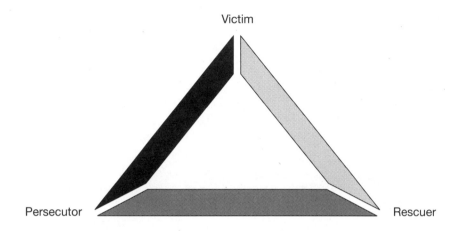

Figure 4.2 The Drama Triangle

The drama triangle involves interaction between two or more people. Often one person, playing one of these roles, implicitly invites someone to play another role. So, for example, a facilitator in a compulsive rescuer role will often look for a victim to rescue and a group member will conveniently fill the victim role. The roles are repetitive, compulsive and carried out unconsciously. Karpman describes these roles as *inauthentic*, meaning that when people are in one of these roles, they are responding to unaware patterns of behaviour from the past rather than to the conscious decision making of the 'here and now'. At any point between people in these positions, there may be a switch where one or both facilitators change to another position.

EXAMPLE

Neville had been a co-facilitator for over four years with Wayne. Neville had more experience as a facilitator. When asked to give feedback by Wayne, he constantly gave negative feedback (playing the Persecutor role) to Wayne. Wayne (playing the victim) accepted the feedback for two years, complaining in secret to his friends about Neville. Eventually Wayne became fed up with the negative feedback and became very angry with Neville, remonstrating about his negativity and about his persecutory attitude (hence himself switching to a persecutor role and thus inviting Neville to move to a victim role).

The victim position in co-facilitation is a one-down position. It tends to take the form of one facilitator feeling like the other trainer has worked against them in some way or other. Sometimes this is on a one-to-one basis, but it can also involve others, such as the victim facilitator feeling like the co-facilitator is working with the group against them. The key point here is that the facilitator believes this is happening. In reality it may or it may not be, but the facilitator will behave as if it were true, therefore having a detrimental effect on the relationship.

'I know nothing'

In this situation one or other facilitator sees themselves as less knowledgeable/skilled in relation to the other facilitator in all aspects of their work. It is as if they consider all parts of themselves as being less, including their opinions, views and experiences, rather than just that part of them which may indeed be less in comparison to their co-facilitator. Neither do they recognize where they may be more skilled or able than their co-facilitator. It seems to be an 'all or nothing ' position to put themselves in.

--- **EXAMPLE** ---

A group of skilled trainers were asked to work with two more experienced trainers on a series of programmes. They were nervous both about the programmes and about working with the other trainers. During the events they behaved in a way which negated their views, skills, opinions and experience, totally. In reality their skills and knowledge were highly suited to the programme but, in their nervousness, they seemed to forget their own skills. In doing this they behaved as if they knew nothing of use to the programmes and gave all their power away to the more experienced trainers, becoming very dependent on them, and 'swallowing down' anything they said as absolute truth.

'I'm just here to learn'

This is where one facilitator explains their role as being junior facilitator to the other, and is therefore a one-down power position. They see their main purpose as being 'there to learn'. In practice this often means that they discount their own views and skills and use the other facilitator as a role model for everything they do, swallowing down whole everything the other facilitator does and says as correct. Swallowing down whole has an interesting explanation in Gestalt psychology, in which it is called introjecting. Gestalt psychology defines this as 'accepting information or values from the outside without evaluation'. Although this dynamic is only one example of introjection, it does serve to show how, when out of awareness, it can have a negative effect on the co-facilitative relationship.

The above examples are only three of the most common one-down dynamics. There are many others.

REFLECTION

▶ Consider the times you have co-facilitated or trained. In what ways were either of you in a one-down position?
▶ What part did you play in contributing to this dynamic?
▶ If you could give a label to this dynamic what would it be called?
▶ With hindsight, what needs would you say were being met by yourself and your co-facilitator?
▶ How else might you get those needs met?
▶ What other one-down positions can you think of?

One-up

Our definition of the one-up dynamic is when a facilitator perceives themselves as being in a 'higher' position than their co-facilitator, using whatever criteria they choose. They then behave in a way which reinforces this view of themselves.

There are again many ways in which this can and does happen. To illustrate the point we have picked out some of the most common ways in which we have seen this happen in practice. The examples we outline here are as follows:

- Rescuer
- Persecutor
- Rationalization
- Delegator.

Rescuer (or 'Don't worry, I'll look after you')

As in the Drama Triangle discussed earlier, this position when taken by a co-facilitator is a one-up power position. It is a one-up position because the basic assumption taken by the facilitator is that they know better than the person they are rescuing (in this case their co-facilitator) or have more skills than them to the extent that they need to look after their co-facilitator. Although it may be done in all good intent, a consequence of doing this out of awareness is that it sets up a process dynamic in which there is an imbalance of power.

In practical terms this can take the form of one facilitator protecting the other from the group, speaking for the other facilitator, doing the co-facilitator's sessions for them, among many other behavioural examples.

EXAMPLE

Ellen, John and Adelle were running a group for experienced trainers. Ellen had introduced an activity designed to help the group explore aspects of their groupwork. The group became hostile to Ellen and started to attack her and the activity. Although Ellen was an experienced facilitator and capable of dealing with the dynamic, John jumped into defending both Ellen and the activity, without allowing Ellen the opportunity of dealing with the issue herself. This protection resulted in the group perceiving Ellen as less competent than her co-facilitators.

Persecutor (or 'I'll get you whatever you do')

This dynamic is where one facilitator persecutes or puts down another facilitator, therefore keeping themselves in a one-up position. The perpetual persecutor will find any way of remaining in a one-up position by putting down their co-facilitator. This may be done explicitly or implicitly, obviously or subtly. This happens in a number of ways, sometimes in a direct way, such as siding with the group against the other facilitator, or directly, putting down on a one to one basis between the two facilitators. It can also happen in less direct ways such as sabotage, ignoring, manipulating and discounting.

EXAMPLE

George and Anne were running a workshop on cultural change. Whenever George gave an explanation of some theory or introduced an activity, Anne supplemented this (unnecessarily) by saying things like 'What George means is…' or 'Perhaps you would also like to look at…'. Also, while George was speaking, Anne often had a frown of disapproval on her face. George felt constantly undermined.

Rationalization (or 'It's all because you're here')

This dynamic is where the one-up facilitator blames anything that does not go 'right' on the presence of the other facilitator. This allows the facilitator to believe that they are better in some shape or form. Often they are very skilled at explaining how the other facilitator has a link to the issue. In our research we even came across a situation where the facilitator had managed to convince themselves of this dynamic even when the co-facilitator was not present! On a process level what this does is usually maintain a power relationship of one-up, one-down.

EXAMPLE

Marina had a clear view about what learning should be gained from the use of a particular exercise. When Fred introduced the exercise, and the group carried it out, they explored some different issues from those which Marina had expected. Marina therefore felt that the exercise had failed and held Fred's introduction as responsible for this.

Delegation (or 'It will be good for you')

This dynamic is when one facilitator considers themselves to be responsible for the development of the other facilitator. This can take many forms and one of these is where one facilitator considers anything that they have been through to be the development the other facilitator should go through. With this in mind they often 'delegate' work to their other facilitator and, of course, this is 'For their own good'. The one-up position is one in which they consider they know the development needs of their co-facilitator better than the co-facilitator themselves.

REFLECTION

▶   Considering your co-facilitation experiences, when have you been in a one-up position?

▶   What did you do to contribute to this dynamic?

▶   If you could give this dynamic a label or name, what would it be?

▶   What needs were being met by you and your co-facilitator?

▶   How else might you get these needs met?

▶   What other one-up power positions can you think of?

Awareness or unawareness?

One key to whether any of these dynamics works for or against your co-facilitative practice is the awareness of each facilitator. Let's face it, none of us are exactly equal to everyone else (thank goodness!). Each of us will be 'better' at some things and 'worse' at others, therefore with anyone else we can be in a one-up or one-down position. We therefore all have the ability to be in either of these power positions.

Within awareness, then, power positions are not necessarily a bad thing. If we are aware then we have a choice as to whether to remain in that position or not, it is not habitual and this awareness gives us choice. We might get many needs met in either of these positions. For example, in a one-down position each of us may allow ourselves to receive coaching and learn from someone with greater knowledge or skills in a particular area. We may also allow ourselves to follow when we decide that leading or even taking joint responsibility is not so appropriate. In a one-up position we may allow ourselves to meet other needs we have such as our recognition and self-esteem needs.

Being in an effective co-facilitative relationship does not necessarily mean being equal. Many of the most effective pieces of co-facilitation that we have seen have been done by a pair that are not equal. The key seems to be that, in the most effective relationships, they are aware of the dynamic and have choice around it. Power is perceived as flexible rather than fixed, and it shifts between the facilitators according to the demands of the situation and their particular skills.

Many dysfunctional co-facilitative relationships have an unaware dynamic around power positions. One party perceive themselves in relation to the other in a way they are unhappy with. This often seems to surface in either general dissatisfaction which is not focused on any one particular issue or with anger towards the other facilitator. In such cases facilitators are not aware of what is really happening on a process level or what their real needs are.

EXAMPLE

Phil was doing a piece of co-facilitation for a group of other trainers. After a while he asked for some feedback about how he was perceived by the group. The feedback was that he seemed to be taking a junior position to Lee, his co-facilitator. He did not like this as it was a long term issue that he had been trying to address over the past year. Even so he took the feedback without responding to the group. His internal response was to blame the group for not 'allowing' him to break out of the junior position. He also went very quiet for the rest of the programme and quietly seethed about the feedback. At the end of the programme he felt angry that neither the group nor the other facilitator, Lee, had noticed how quiet he was and done something about it. Lee had deliberately not responded to Phil's 'sulking' (as he saw it).

- What is happening here?
- What clues have you got about the power position of Phil?
- What could have Phil and Lee have done differently?

ACTIVITY

1. Working with a co-facilitator, imagine a continuum or line on the floor across the room. The continuum is split into four broad parts (see Figure 4.3). This continuum is about power. Start at one end by actually standing on the start of the line.

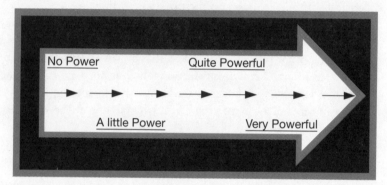

Figure 4.3   Power continuum

2. This end represents you, when you are feel you have no power. Close your eyes and stand in this position. Your partner can now start to ask you what it is like to be in this position. It may be that you are experiencing a memory, a feeling, thought or even a physical sensation. Describe to your partner whatever happens to you. Take your time over this.

3. Now take a step to a third of the way along the line. This represents you when you have a little power. Your partner can now take you through the same steps as before, as you describe what happens to you when you are like this.

4. Repeat the step for:

   (a) Two-thirds along the continuum (for feeling quite powerful);

   (b) At the end of the continuum (for feeling very powerful).

5. Now discuss the following questions.

▶   What are the most significant changes in you, when you move from being less to more powerful?

▶   What are the triggers that move you into a less or more powerful position?

▶   What are the implications for you as a co-facilitator?

▶   What can your co-facilitator do to help you maintain your power?

PROJECTION

The second major dynamic that occurs between co-facilitators is that of projection. This concept is drawn both from Gestalt psychology and from psychoanalysis. It can be described as: 'Attributing to your co-facilitator, thoughts, feelings and behaviours which are actually part of yourself.' In this sense, then, projection is a confusion between what is part of ourselves and what is part of our co-facilitator.

When co-facilitators work together there are numbers of projections going on at an unaware level. This is a normal process for all humans and therefore is not necessarily a negative thing. It does, however, play a main part in the relationship between the two facilitators.

ACTIVITY

1. Next time you meet anyone whom you have not met before, write down your answers to the following questions:

   ▶ What type of person are they?

   ▶ How do they normally behave?

   ▶ What are they feeling?

2. Now look at what you have written down, in what ways do these remarks apply to *you*?

3. What gave you the clues about the answers to the question about what type of person they are? (Was it the way they look, or an expression, their clothes, or the way they speak?)

The theory of projection states that we only see in others what we have in ourselves. Many people find this hard to accept as we often project the parts of ourselves which we do not want to recognize or own, but this is happening at an unaware level, and so is not something that we would notice as going on. So how does projection work? When we see 'clues' in other people we unconsciously try and make sense of them from our own experience of the world. In practice this means that how someone looks, how they are dressed, a non-verbal movement, a word or sentence, may immediately trigger a projection in us about that person. Assumptions we make about people are one way of projecting.

Projections may be positive or negative. For example, we can just as easily project confidence on to someone as we can nervousness. Therefore projection is the tendency to find an external host for what originates in the self. An example is the facilitator who likes to be patient with their co-facilitator, but cannot stand the co-facilitator always wanting them to hurry on to the next activity. The facilitator here is likely to be unaware of their own impatience and is projecting it on to their co-facilitator. This in turn makes it hard to deal with the co-facilitator. Sometimes our projections may actually turn out to be truly a part of the other person as well as ourselves. It is worth checking out your projections to see how accurate they are.

ACTIVITY

With your co-facilitator, take it in turns to answer the following:

1. I am like you in these ways…

2. I am different from you in these ways…

3. What I imagine you think about me is…

4. What I imagine about you is…

Now discuss what you have learnt about yourself and your co-facilitator.

TRANSFERENCE

The third major dynamic occurring between co-facilitators is called transference. Transference can be described as 'reacting to someone as if they are a significant person from your past'. This significant person may be a parent, relative, teacher, friend or anyone whom you had contact as a child and who had an impact on you at the time. Often we have forgotten this person or the particular incidents that had an impact on us then. What we do retain, however, is the emotional response that we had, and how we learnt to respond at the time to the person and the situation.

One very common example of this in organizations is the response to senior managers. Do you find yourself responding to senior managers in a more submissive way than normal? Or maybe you find yourself responding in a more challenging way than normal? Either way something about the manager has triggered off a response in you. This response is the response that you had when you were a child to a senior figure (often a parent or teacher). It is not that these responses are chosen and within awareness, but they have long since moved into unawareness. When we were children they made perfect sense as responses, for example to be submissive to parents and teachers was probably a good choice of response at the time. However, the key word here is 'choice', the difference being that in adult life such a response often stops becoming a choice, as we act out of awareness and automatically, so it may not be our best response.

ACTIVITY

A common time for transference is at the beginning of training programmes.

Think about one event you have been involved in. What initial behaviours did you notice in yourself and in others, in response to the trainers or facilitators? Note down some of the responses and behaviours you observed.

Now notice how some of those behaviours are childlike responses. As the programme moves on, notice how the responses change, and as the transferences start to dissipate, notice how people start to make more choices over their responses and behaviours.

Some common transferential responses in such situations are as follows.

▶   'The perfect delegate' or 'Look how good I am Daddy'.

▶   'I'll challenge you' or 'Give me some attention'.

▶   'Coy' or 'But I'm shy'.

▶   'Delegates just want to have fun' or 'It's playtime'.

▶   'I'll stick up for you' or 'I'll protect you, Mum/Dad'.

Of course, in practice, there are many types of transference; in fact, each person is likely to have their own transferential responses.

ACTIVITY

Take it in turns to carry out the following steps.

1. Spend a few minutes considering your co-facilitator.

2. Who do they remind you of?

3. In what ways are they like this person?

4. In what ways are they unlike this person?

5. In what ways are you treating them as if they are someone else?

6. How will your behaviour towards your co-facilitator change now?

VALUES AND OBJECTIVES

Another major area of process that co-facilitators can examine is that of values and beliefs. If you believe that behaviours are a consequence of our values and beliefs, then understanding and hopefully aligning the beliefs and values between co-facilitators can be useful. This is not to say that we all need to have the same values and beliefs, far from it, but conflicting values and beliefs are often at the root of problems in a co-facilitative relationship.

Obviously everyone has many different values and beliefs. In co-facilitation of particular importance are the values and beliefs around learning, our role in this and the amount of control and directiveness we should have in the learning process.

REFLECTION

At a recent co-facilitated event, here are some of the most common things that each facilitator said to the group.

Facilitator 1

'So what can you learn from that?'

'Tell me more about what you just said.'

'What else happened?'

'How does this relate to what normally happens with you?'

'What would it be useful to do next?'

'So you seem to be saying that...'

Facilitator 2

'Don't forget that...'

'This is what is most important here.'

'Don't you think that...'

'This means that...'

'I think that now we will...'

'You need to...'

'So what you mean is...'

From these typical responses from each facilitator, what would you guess are some of the different beliefs and values that they hold around learning? What might be the effect on their co-facilitative practice?

ACTIVITY: DISCOVERING VALUES

Do this exercise as a pair. Decide who will speak first, and then go through the following steps.

1. One facilitator talks about the people that they admire in the field of training or facilitation.

2. The co-facilitator asks 'What is it about these people that you admire?' The co-facilitator asks 'Why is that quality significant for you?'

3. The co-facilitator then feeds back to their partner from the above answers, what they would see as their partner's values.

4. Both discuss the values emerging for the facilitator from this exercise and how these influence their practice.

5. Repeat steps 1 to 4 with the other facilitator.

6. How are your values similar or different, and how will you work with this?

Reviewing group exercises as co-facilitators

We believe that behaviour can reflect values. So values and beliefs display themselves in reviewing exercises with the group. This is one area where differences of values and beliefs are important.

In your reviewing, what is the basic belief or value that each of you is working from? Here are two examples.

- 'I am here to teach you something – what I want you to learn.'
- 'I am here to review what happened and see what learning emerges.'

All this is essential to how the reviews are run, in fact much more important than any techniques. With the example quoted above in the reflection on page 65, the statements made by each facilitator give us some clues about their values and beliefs regarding learning and facilitation. Either could be 'right', that is not the point. The point is that they were operating unawarely out of different values and beliefs. If you were a delegate on this programme, what would be your response to these? We have found that it often serves to confuse and hinder learning for delegates when co-facilitators have vastly different beliefs or values.

AWARENESS OF SIMILARITIES AND DIFFERENCES

ACTIVITY

1. Consider a facilitator you have worked with. In what ways are they different from you? Write these down.

2. Looking at the list you have written, mark against each difference which of these are helpful and which you find a hindrance, being as honest as you can.

3. Now look at those you have labelled as a hindrance. In what ways could these be used to make them helpful rather than a hindrance?

Our research showed that there are inevitable differences between facilitators. The difference between this being helpful or not is how these differences are understood, accepted and used to benefit the co-facilitative practice.

In many less effective co-facilitative relationships, differences are viewed as a nuisance and something to be avoided at all costs. This often results either in a separation of the two facilitators so that the event turns into one split into 'sessions' done separately by each facilitator or into an uneasy mid-point between the differences of the facilitators.

In many highly effective co-facilitative relationships, the differences are viewed as rich sources of learning both for the facilitators and the group, which are to be accepted, explored and used to build on the strengths of each. This often results in facilitators working together with a group in utilizing their own strengths and learning from those of their co-facilitator. This can be difficult, but the group can benefit greatly from the different approaches, and from seeing positive modelling of an approach to working with and gaining from difference.

ACTIVITY

1. Individually, write down any areas of similarity and difference between you and your co-facilitator. This might include your approach, your personal aims or anything else which comes to mind. (Probably what comes to mind straight away or what is 'on top' is the most important at this time.)

2. As a pair discuss your perceptions from number 1. How do your perceptions compare with those of your co-facilitator?

3. What are the implications for you as co-facilitators? What are your key insights?

MEETING NEEDS

Each co-facilitator has a set of needs which they are aiming to meet (these needs may be in or out of awareness). Some of these needs will be met by the group, but each co-facilitator will also look to their relationship with them to meet some of these needs.

One of the common dynamics we have come across between co-facilitators is that of needs not being shared and dissatisfaction arising out of this.

One facilitator told a story about how they worked alongside someone who was subsequently very angry with them. Apparently they had spent a lot of time contracting and agreeing outcomes, and sharing what each of them wanted from the programme. Only after the programme did the co-facilitator express their disappointment that first the facilitators had not 'convinced' the group to change their practice in one particular area and secondly that they had not become 'friends' with the group. Neither of these needs had been stated before or during the groupwork. This is a good example of how not working and sharing needs can be dysfunctional to the co-facilitative practice. It is for this reason why clear contracting and continuous reviewing of needs is so important.

Some needs will be clear before working together, but also some needs will emerge during the work, which is why interim co-facilitative reviews are very important. You can also take your developing awareness of your needs with you into different co-facilitative relationships.

ACTIVITY

1. Using a model (such as Maslow's or Herzberg's) to help you identify your needs, each facilitator writes down the needs that they have in relation to working as a co-facilitator on this piece of work.

2. Discuss the needs on each of the lists. How do you normally get these needs met?

3. What needs are similar between you?

4. What needs are different?

5. In meeting your needs, how might you prevent your co-facilitator from meeting their needs?

6. What would you like your co-facilitator to do in order for you to get your needs met?

(Note: You might like to use Figure 4.4 below to carry out the above exercise.)

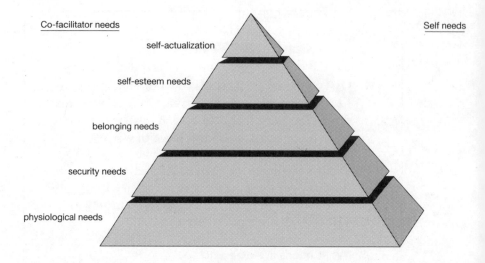

Co-facilitator needs   Self needs

self-actualization

self-esteem needs

belonging needs

security needs

physiological needs

Figure 4.4   Comparing co-facilitator needs using Maslow's Hierarchy of Needs

QUALITY OF CONTACT

What would you say is the quality of contact between you and your co-facilitator? A key aspect of the effectiveness of your co-facilitative practice is the quality of contact between you.

Levels of contact

Contact is a term describing the quality of interaction between a person and the environment around them. This environment includes other people in contact with the person, such as co-facilitators and group members. There are various levels of contact between facilitators, as set out below.

Level 1. Social level

At this level of contact the interaction between co-facilitators tends to be on a social level. On this level the interactions are social, clichéd, and often ritualistic. This includes the pleasantries and niceties that many of us go through with others on a daily basis.

When contact remains at this level the awareness and understanding also tends to stay at this level. It is, however, also often a necessary level of interaction in order to move to a deeper, more contactful level.

Level 2. Role/task level

At this level of contact the interactions are generally around the task or roles that co-facilitators play in the task. This includes many of the issues concerning the practicalities of the work discussed in Chapter 3. Many co-facilitative partnerships we have come across work mainly within this level of contact.

Some typical types of contact between co-facilitators at this level would be reviewing the work done; discussing the content; planning the design of events and intervention styles.

Level 3. Interpersonal level

At this level of contact the interaction between the co-facilitators is around the relationship between them. The focus of attention is what is happening or has happened on an interpersonal level.

Some typical types of contact between co-facilitators would include feedback to each other; discussion of reactions towards each other; feelings towards each other during the work; shared or different values and beliefs; expectations of each other.

Level 4. Personal level

At this level of contact, the interaction between facilitators is based on the personal processes of each facilitator. This is an in-depth level of contact, and is often a contact which brings raised awareness and new discoveries. The focus of attention is around how the relationships and the task enable personal awareness, development and learning to take place.

Typical contact between co-facilitators may include such things as personal motivation; values and beliefs; personalities.

The following activity is a start point to beginning to build the relationship on a deeper level than the social level. Each facilitator should complete the activity separately, and then come together to share and discuss answers. This in itself will help you start to work at deeper levels of contact.

REFLECTION

► Consider a piece of co-facilitation you have recently carried out.
► Think about the contact between you and your co-facilitator.
► At what level do you see most of the contact between the two of you happening?
► What is *not* being discussed in this relationship?

(Note: It is often what is not being said that can give us clues as to how to develop the relationship and practice further.)

The following activity is a start point to beginning to build the relationship on a deeper level than the social level. Each facilitator completes the activity separately, and then come together to share and discuss answers. This in itself will help you to start work at deeper levels of contact.

ACTIVITY: 'LET'S LEARN ABOUT EACH OTHER'

1. Learning approach
Write a statement of about 100 words to explain your concept of how people learn.

2. Personal motivation
Complete the following sentence: 'I am involved in training/facilitation because...'

3. Expectations
What things do you expect to happen in this group?
What would be the best/worst thing that could happen?

4. Intervention style
Usual responses:
'When starting the group, I usually...'
'When the group is quiet, I usually...'
'When a group member gets upset or cries, I usually...'
'When someone is late or interrupts the group, I usually...'
'When there is an attack on one individual in the group I usually...'
'When there is conflict in the group, I usually...'
'When someone flirts with me in the group I usually...'

5. Other interventions
'My favourite types of interventions are...'
'My typical pace/speed is...'
'My style tends to be... (nurturing/confronting/friendly/distant etc)
'The thing that makes me most uncomfortable in groups is...'

6. Talk through your responses with your co-facilitator

There are many differences in each co-facilitative relationship. However, research shows that there are a number of common dynamics which significantly contribute to the quality of the relationship and contact between co-facilitators. These include the following.

1. *Willingness to learn and change.* Within the relationship, what are you willing to change, and what are you *not* willing to change? Are you approaching the work with a genuine view of learning for yourself?

2. *Interest in the co-facilitation.* The fact that you are reading this probably indicates that you are interested in making your co-facilitative practice better! However, all of the dynamics in this chapter rely on the fact that both facilitators have an interest in making their practice work and building on it.

3. *Balance of support and challenge.* Within the work, an important element seems to be the knowledge that your co-facilitator will support you when you need support. This is not just giving support, but the knowledge and belief by each facilitator that support is available from their co-facilitator. In balance to this, challenge seems to be an essential part of the development process of the co-facilitation.

4. *Ability and willingness to recognize and utilize differences.* As stated above, there will be differences between you and your co-facilitators. It is not only important to recognize what these differences are, but it is also important how these differences are used. In your co-facilitation, are these differences considered as a problem to be controlled and dealt with? Or are the differences considered to be useful dynamics which may lead to development of the co-facilitative relationship?

5. *A bringing of the 'whole' person (not just the facilitator).* We believe that the most successful co-facilitative relationships encompass the whole person. Many co-facilitators seem to keep one part of themselves separate from the work. Often the parts of each facilitator which may not seem directly related to the work can add greatly to the quality of the relationship, and this in turn will impact on the work undertaken.

THE CO-FACILITATORS' ENVIRONMENT

When you and your co-facilitator meet and work together, you will have each come from your own respective background and environment. The assumption here is often that this environment can be ignored in the context of what is happening now, but in reality a meeting of two facilitators is also a meeting of their respective environments.

Gestalt theory refers to 'the field' and field theory. The field is all the coexisting mutually interdependent factors of a person and their environment. Their experiences, culture, social background, family situation, history, other relationships and many other areas, form together to make the 'person' as we experience them. The person as a 'whole' is affected by a change in any one of these.

A good metaphor for this effect is the body: if I pull a muscle in my shoulder, other muscles in my body will compensate by contracting and my overall posture is likely to be affected. At the same time, my pain may also make me irritable and I become offhand with my colleagues, thus affecting my working relationships. This example shows how a change in one part of my 'field' can have an impact on other parts of me.

In the same way, if my experiences of good development have always been painful, then I bring that to the design work I might carry out with a co-facilitator and attempt to pass that on to participants in the programme. When, however, I might work with a co-facilitator who has learnt nothing from painful experiences, these parts of our 'fields' are very different.

Within each of our 'fields', we will be aware of some things more at a particular time and others at different times. We tend to focus on one thing at a time and this is called the 'figure'. The background environment does not stop influencing us, but it is not foremost in our minds.

In co-facilitation, our 'figure' is often the work and the relationship between us, but the other field influences are still in play and therefore it is good to be aware of them. The background to your co-facilitation may well be what holds the key to success in your co-facilitation.

ACTIVITY: UNDERSTANDING YOUR FIELD

1. Take 30 minutes each to think about your life story, up to and including today. If you were to tell your story in 15 minutes, what would you say?

2. Now find somewhere where you will not be interrupted and tell your co-facilitator your story.

3. At the end, ask your co-facilitator to feedback to you: what stands out for them from your story?

SUMMARY

In any co-facilitative practice, there are two broad areas within the relationship. These areas are the content level and the process level. Both areas need to be worked on and developed to achieve excellence in co-facilitative practice.

This chapter outlined the process level of working with your co-facilitative practice. There are a number of key dynamics outlined here.

Power positions

Power positions are the dynamics of the relationship in terms of power and perceived power. The common patterns of relationships that form in terms of power and how each facilitator may play a part in sustaining unaware patterns of power. Power positions are often out of awareness and there tends to be one facilitator being in a one-up position, while the other is in a one-down position.

Projection

This is the process by which we project our own thoughts, feelings, values, beliefs and behaviours on to our co-facilitators. Having done this we then act as if these were true. Projections can be positive or negative, and once projected they can become a self-fulfilling prophecy in that we treat co-facilitators as if our projections are true, and hence they act 'into' this projection.

Transference

This is a type of projection where we treat someone as if they were someone else. This is an unconscious process and may be triggered off by a voice, a word, a look, a non-verbal or an expression in our co-facilitator. The danger is that they are not the other person and so our transferences are not accurate. We can then act on this false information by treating the co-facilitator as if our transferences were true.

Values and objectives

Values and objectives often form the basis of the behaviour of co-facilitators, and hence are a key process on which to work. There are some key base values that will need to be understood, such as beliefs around learning and people. There may be others, but, awareness of them between you and your co-facilitator can be developmental for the relationship and practice.

Similarities and differences

There will be similarities and differences between you and your co-facilitator. In itself this is not as important as being aware of these, and learning as a pair to work on them, understand and utilize them.

Meeting needs

Each facilitator will bring their own needs to the co-facilitative relationship. Some of these needs will be within awareness, some out of awareness. Whatever the needs are, each facilitator will look to their co-facilitator to help meet these needs. They need therefore to be explicitly worked on as part of the co-facilitative relationship.

Quality of contact

Within each relationship, there will be patterns of contact. There are various depths of contact and these patterns will reflect the depth of working together. The deeper the contact the more developmental the contact is likely to be. This section outlines the levels of contact.

Above are some of the most common dynamics that we have come across in our practice and our research into co-facilitation. However, this is not meant to be an exhaustive list. It will be useful for you to discover your own processes and add to our list.

All of the above processes are at an unaware level. They go on for all of us every day in all our lives, so don't immediately fear the worst. These are not pathological illnesses! The purpose of this chapter is to enable you to raise your awareness about the dynamics which will already be going on in your co-facilitative relationships. We find that when people really discover the world of process (as opposed to talking about it), there is often a 'Columbus effect'. That is, suddenly someone discovers that the world is not a flat or black and white one of content and practical arrangements between co-facilitators. Instead they discover that the world is round, colourful, dynamic, and one of change and excitement.

5

Development of the Co-facilitative Relationship

We begin this chapter with a look at whether or not potential co-facilitators should be able to choose if they work together and explore how they might make this decision, as well as examining its practical implications. We then go on to examine the importance of the relationship between co-facilitators and put forward the case, based on our research as well as our own experience, for paying attention to how this can most effectively be developed. An overview of our model, outlining the different developmental stages through which a co-facilitative relationship tends to go, is then introduced. We then take an in depth look at each of the stages identified. At each stage we have included opportunities for reflection designed to help you to review your co-facilitative practice and, if possible, to aid your progression through the stages. We hope you will start to gain plenty of ideas for developing your own co-facilitative practice as a result of reading and working through this chapter. More detailed practical help on how to achieve this is given in Chapter 6.

CHOOSING A CO-FACILITATOR

We start with an exploration of whether it is desirable to have choice about your co-facilitator, since this is likely to influence the relationship in positive or negative ways from its onset. From our review of the (highly limited) literature focusing on co-facilitation, Corey and Corey (1992) express a clear preference for what they term co-leading and assert the importance of choosing to work with colleagues whom you respect and trust. However, the results of our research showed that this question of choice was a complex one, which provoked strong and differing views. Some were clearly in favour of choosing their co-facilitators:

'I think the best co-facilitation happens when the people themselves decide to work together.'

'There are some people whom I could never work with. This seems more about a conflicting world view or values than personal style.'

As indicated, this preference was based on potential co-facilitators having a similar or shared philosophy, values and beliefs. It was this bedrock which then allowed differences, particularly of facilitation style, to be not merely accommodated but utilized and valued. As one co-facilitator expressed it:

'Our values and beliefs about developmental training are very similar. Our styles are different and complement each other.'

We support the view implied here that the important similarities lie in the core area of values while co-facilitator differences are often peripheral and behavioural, but more easily perceived and recognized by group members as providing a source of added value. Our own experience as co-facilitators supports this. Some of our most effective co-facilitation has been with people who have quite different attributes, experiences and personalities from our own, but who share some common beliefs about the purpose and value of facilitation in enabling learning and about the learning process itself. Conversely, without this shared bedrock of understanding, we have found ourselves trying to achieve different outcomes in inconsistent ways – which has limited our effectiveness as co-facilitators and adversely impacted on the work being undertaken.

However, an alternative view about the importance of choice regarding co-facilitators was also expressed. We have some evidence that choice is not always important or even, maybe, desirable. For example, one interviewee spoke of a high initial uncertainty about the prospect of working with a particular facilitator, though they then went on to develop what she characterized as one of her most successful co-facilitative relationships. This view, which questions the importance of choice, may also be a pragmatic response to the common lack of or limited choice regarding the people we work with, both in co-facilitation and more generally. For many facilitators working in organizations there is little freedom of choice regarding their co-facilitators, as these are typically colleagues operating within the same organization and it may be practically or culturally unacceptable to choose not to work with them. Even as an external consultant, there can be limited opportunity to influence this choice as clients wish to develop their own skills by working alongside a perceived 'expert', and enabling their professional development can form part of the working approach and methods outlined in the contract for the assignment. As the choice of co-facilitator is so frequently limited, we may take a pragmatic position and limit our perception of the degree of importance attached to the decision.

These differing views raise some interesting questions. How do we decide whether or not we can work effectively with someone, especially when we may have very limited knowledge of them? How do we know whether or not our judgement is sound? Do we sometimes set up self-fulfilling prophecies which tend to reinforce us in our original viewpoint? Do we miss out on opportunities to learn from people who may challenge us by their different viewpoints if we always choose our co-facilitators?

REFLECTION

▶ Have you typically exercised choice regarding your co-facilitators?

▶ On what basis did you make a decision to work together or not?

▶ Can you identify any link between choosing a co-facilitator and the subsequent degree of effectiveness of your working relationship?

▶ Where you felt you had no choice regarding a co-facilitator, how do you believe this affected your subsequent relationship (if at all)?

Making an informed choice

We believe that it is preferable to be able to exercise some degree of choice regarding your co-facilitators, but that the validity of making such a choice is dependent on its being an informed decision – by which we mean that you have clarity regarding the criteria affecting your decision and that these are relevant to effective co-facilitation. Otherwise, it is possible that you may limit your own learning and development by only working with people for whom you quickly feel some affinity. Reflecting on our past experiences of co-facilitation, we have sometimes gained the most learning by working with people to whom, initially, we did not feel intuitively attracted – precisely because of their difference from ourselves.

Our experience and our research have both shown that there are some areas where it seems to be important, in terms of the future effectiveness of the working relationship, for co-facilitators to share similarities. These are indicated in Figure 5.1 where the areas of darkest shading show where it is appropriate and important to have greatest co-facilitator similarity. The prime area where there is a need for similarity lies in the basic philosophy and values which influence the way in which each facilitator works, whether they are aware of this or not. It is this bedrock of shared or similar values which seems to allow differences, particularly of facilitator style, to be not merely accommodated but also utilized and valued. However, where this bedrock does not exist, then co-facilitators can find themselves working to achieve different outcomes in ways which are fundamentally different – if not directly opposed.

Conversely, there are other aspects of facilitation where differences are required between co-facilitators in order for them to offer more opportunities for learning and provide groups with a source of added value. These areas, indicated in Figure 5.1 by the areas of lighter shading, are those which relate to more superficial (though nevertheless important) facilitator behaviours which may be those differences most easily perceived by client groups. As co-facilitators involved in our research expressed it:

'What works best with co-facilitation is when there's somehow a good proportion of those similarities plus those differences.'

'Our values and beliefs about developmental training are very similar. Our styles are quite different and complement each other.'

It seems clear that a mixture of similarities and differences between co-facilitators produces the most effective working relationships, but that certain areas of similarity are important in contributing to viable co-facilitation.

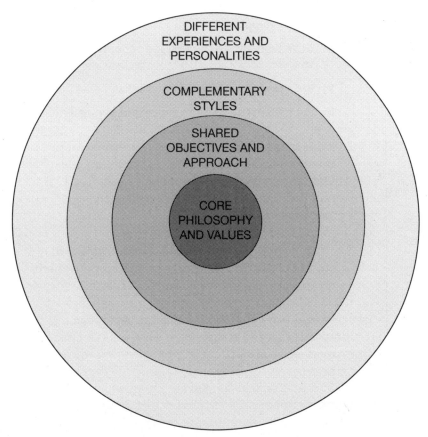

Figure 5.1   Dimensions of co-facilitator similarity and difference

Using this information, you can develop a means of exploring whether or not it will be appropriate to work with a particular co-facilitator. Below are some further guidelines to help you.

ACTIVITY

1. What questions will you want to ask a potential co-facilitator in order to find out about:

   ▶ their philosophy and values concerning learning and development;

   ▶ their objectives and intended approach to the specific work project under discussion;

   ▶ their preferred style as a facilitator;

   ▶ their background, experience and personality?

2. How confident and able are you to answer these questions about yourself? For example, are you clear about the values that influence your work? If not, how can you gain a better understanding of the way in which you work?

3. What do you see as the particular strengths and attributes that you bring to your facilitation? Where do you lack experience or have weaknesses?

4. In what ways could a co-facilitator best provide added value and complement what you can bring to the specific project under discussion?

The practical implications

Whether you have complete freedom of choice regarding your prospective co-facilitators or not, it is important that you utilize the opportunity to find out about each other prior to engaging in work together. In this way, you can start to identify how you might work most effectively together, taking account of your current understanding of your areas of similarity and difference. Our research showed that choosing a co-facilitator was less important than having the skills and willingness to explore and resolve any issues which arose between co-facilitators, since an initial liking for someone did not mean that no difficulties were likely to arise in the relationship. However, if there is no shared bedrock of similar values, it may be more tempting to abandon a difficult working relationship in favour of ones that seem to be more potentially fruitful. There is likely to be a lack of commitment to that relationship and this may result in its termination at an early opportunity.

In the worst case, such an exploration can help you to decide, using relevant criteria, that it would risk the outcomes of the project if you were to work together. Although we understand that it can be difficult to refuse to work with a colleague, being able to present coherent reasons for this in terms of the likely impact on the level of success of the project, is a much more credible argument than citing an instinctive dislike or unease.

THE IMPORTANCE OF THE CO-FACILITATIVE RELATIONSHIP

Before we examine how the relationship between co-facilitators develops, it may be useful to state why we consider that paying attention to this is so important if you are to work at a high level of competence as a co-facilitator. We have already commented on the 'taken-for-granted' nature of co-facilitation, whereby there seems to be a working assumption that 'if you can facilitate, then you can also co-facilitate'. This taken-for-granted aspect of co-facilitation led us to liken it to marriage, as couples often seem to enter into marriage on the basis of a physical and intuitive attraction, ignoring the fact that their relationship will in all probability also need some hard work if it is to survive and prosper. In a similar way, issues arise between husband and wife which will need to be addressed if the relationship is not to become stagnant, destructive or collusive.

We challenge this working assumption, that co-facilitation needs no special or additional skill, based on our own experience and our research. In many situations, experienced facilitators have found that their effectiveness is limited, to varying degrees, by working with particular co-facilitators. What is interesting is that in many cases they appear not to have given this much thought, until prompted to do so by our research – despite concerns about the quality of the working relationship.

We hope that our examination of the potential benefits and disadvantages of co-facilitation has provided you with some motivation and interest to explore the nature of the relationship between co-facilitators and how this can be developed. We have also described in some detail the main dynamics which we have found to arise between co-facilitators and the adverse impact which these can have on their working relationship when they are acted out unawarely rather than being explored and addressed. However, the fact that these issues exist is not the main cause of co-facilitator ineffectiveness – it is the unwillingness to recognize them and/or the lack of skill to address them.

STAGES OF DEVELOPMENT IN CO-FACILITATOR RELATIONSHIPS

From our research it appears that the relationship between co-facilitators typically goes through three main stages, which we have characterized as:

- the initial stage;
- the developing stage;
- the partnership stage.

Each stage will be described in more detail shortly, but in essence they represent a significant development in terms of the level of effectiveness of the co-facilitative relationship. While each stage builds on the previous one and incorporates some of its positive features, the new stage also represents a qualitative shift in the nature of the working relationship between the co-facilitators. However, it is hard to describe in concrete terms where the boundary separating one stage from another lies and, inevitably, life is never as neat as any model implies.

We should emphasize here that not all co-facilitative relationships will go through all of these stages, as some may be terminated either through choice or circumstance, before they have progressed to the later stages. Others may only ever operate at a relatively low level of effectiveness due to the co-facilitators' limited level of skill or willingness to develop the relationship. Neither can the length of time taken to progress through a particular stage be specified, since this will be determined by the skill level of the facilitators involved in recognizing and dealing with issues which arise between them and by their willingness to engage in this type of exploration. Two factors are critical in moving through the stages:

- the development of an effective co-facilitative relationship requires conscious attention and action by both (all) parties;
- relationships take time to reach a high level of effectiveness.

This model does not present co-facilitators with a simple blueprint which they can follow methodically in order to achieve effectiveness. Any model is, in some way, a simplification of the complexity of our experience. It can help us to make sense of our experience and influence how we respond to similar situations in future, but it needs to be followed in a way which reflects its essence rather than allowing it to be constraining. We therefore recommend that you use this model and the reflections/activities provided here in whichever ways feel most appropriate to you.

The initial stage

This stage begins when potential or newly established co-facilitators start the process of checking each other out in order to make the decision about whether or not to work together or, if they have no choice about this, to explore the basis for their future working together. These early exchanges have the purpose of exploring some or all of the following areas:

- co-facilitators' philosophical beliefs and values concerning learning and development and how best to effect them;
- how they intend to approach the specific project under discussion in order to deliver the desired outcomes;
- their preferred facilitation style and its typical strengths and limitations;
- their individual backgrounds, experiences and personalities.

The overall aim of this exploration is to gain a better understanding of each other although, if this process is undertaken in some depth, facilitators may also learn more about themselves and what is important to them. As a result of this exploration, co-facilitators should be able to ascertain:

- whether there is sufficient similarity in the core areas (philosophy and values) to enable a productive working relationship to be formed;
- what compromises or adjustments need to be made so that they can work effectively together;
- whether it is preferable not to work together.

REFLECTION

▶ What degree of attention have you paid to finding out about new co-facilitators in the past?

▶ Where have you focused your attention? Are there any key areas which you have neglected to explore?

▶ Is there anything which you would want to do differently next time you work with a new co-facilitator?

However, this initial stage can last well beyond the actual beginning of the co-facilitative relationship, as those involved continue to learn about each other and how they can best adjust in order to work together effectively. There will also be a number of practical issues to be discussed and agreed, as the working contract between the co-facilitators is developed. These practicalities have already been examined in Chapter 3, so we shall not explore them further here, other than to note that reaching agreement on these issues can take some time.

While discussions prior to a project being undertaken will help co-facilitators to work well together and avoid some of the potential pitfalls, it is highly unlikely that any early agreements will cover all the eventualities which might occur. There will most likely be a need to review and adjust the working contract over time, by looking at what has been helping and hindering the co-facilitators in working effectively together. Some practical activities to help you to progress your co-facilitative relationships through this stage are given in Chapters 3, 4 and 6.

The transition from the initial to the developing stage is marked by increasing levels of personal disclosure and by more detailed discussions about the interpersonal relationship which exists between the co-facilitators. There is also a more detailed analysis of the work being undertaken and the impact which the co-facilitators are having in terms of helping the group to reach its desired objectives. By the end of the initial stage both (all) co-facilitators are feeling increasingly relaxed in working together, though this does not necessarily mean that there are no difficulties between them. Rather, it signals that they have a growing sense of confidence in their mutual ability to address these, based on the giving and receiving of constructive feedback, and the trust which this disclosure and exchange is building.

When co-facilitators are progressing through this stage in a positive manner, then it tends to be characterized by the following features:

- increased levels of understanding between co-facilitators;
- increasing appreciation of what each can contribute;
- increasing trust;
- exchanges of constructive feedback;
- non-defensive receiving of feedback;
- building on one another's ideas;
- increased levels of openness in communication;
- deeper analysis of the work being undertaken;
- good and clear contracting.

However, where co-facilitators are experiencing difficulties, not just in the work or in their relationship but in their ability to deal with issues arising in these areas, then the initial stage tends to be characterized by the following:

- co-facilitators becoming more fixed in their own individual views;
- increasing concerns about the approach which the other party adopts to the work, and about their individual roles and contributions;
- a tendency to work more independently, where possible, within the parameters of the work;
- emerging competitiveness between co-facilitators;
- decreasing levels of trust;
- reduced level of commitment and interest in working together;
- reduced or low feedback exchange;
- less time spent on reviewing the work undertaken.

It may be useful, especially for those readers who are new to co-facilitation, to give some examples which describe this initial stage of the co-facilitative relationship.

REFLECTION

▶ What signs have indicated to you that you have been moving productively through this stage of the co-facilitative relationship?

▶ How have you become aware that the working relationship is faltering at an early stage of working with a co-facilitator?

▶ Is there any additional action which you could take at an early stage to help new co-facilitative relationships to progress satisfactorily?

CASE STUDY 1

In this case, three co-facilitators were working together on a long-term development programme for trainers and developers which was intended to lead to a post-graduate qualification. They had not worked together previously. Before starting the work, they spent time together to get to know one another and to identify how they would enable participants' learning through the programme. They identified some of their basic values and beliefs concerning learning and development, primarily via a detailed discussion of their thoughts and feelings regarding a Masters level programme on which they had all been participants at different times. They found that they had similar views and feelings about their experience of the programme, and how it might have been improved. This started to create a sense of confidence in a shared approach and in their ability to work together, which each took with them into their initial co-facilitation.

Their understanding of each other was enhanced by the exchange of feedback about their co-facilitation and their feelings about particular sessions. A good level of trust quickly started to develop between all co-facilitators. Soon after they had started working together a potentially difficult situation arose when one facilitator was introducing an activity designed to help participants to explore some group process issues, which was strongly resisted. Although this facilitator was criticized by group members for the design of the activity and his briefing of it, the other co-facilitators did not intervene to help him. After some discussion, the immediate difficulty was resolved and the group engaged in a revised activity. In review, the co-facilitators agreed that interventions from the other two would have been interpreted as 'rescuing' their colleague by group members and that they both had confidence in his ability to resolve the difficulty, as indeed he had done. However, group members initially interpreted their non-intervention as a lack of support for their colleague. This perception provided a useful source of subsequent discussion and learning for all concerned.

REFLECTION

▶ From the description given, how well do you think that these co-facilitators handled the initial stage in their working relationship?

▶ Is there anything else they could have done to help them to progress their working relationship?

▶ What have you learnt from reviewing this case study?

──────────────── **CASE STUDY 2** ────────────────

Two internal consultants, John and Shirley, were about to undertake their first project involving co-facilitation. They agreed the objectives which they wanted to achieve and decided the overall design of the programme. John wanted them each to take individual responsibility for the design and delivery of particular sessions during the programme. Shirley would have preferred to share responsibility for the design process to ensure a higher level of coordination between sessions and to gain a better understanding of each other's facilitation style. However, they each worked separately and delivered the programme sessions with little support and few interventions from each other. Although the intended outcomes were achieved and the participants were pleased with what they had achieved, Shirley felt dissatisfied with their co-facilitation. A brief review to reflect on the work undertaken confirmed that John, however, was quite happy with the outcomes and with the way of working.

REFLECTION

▶ What more could both Shirley and John have done to ensure the success of their co-facilitation?

▶ How do you think that this experience affected their future working relationship?

▶ What can you learn from your review of this case study?

The developing stage

As has already been stated, the transition into this stage of the co-facilitative relationship is characterized by a growing sense of ease, but not necessarily comfort, in working together. The ease comes from the increased understanding which co-facilitators now have of each other, the major influences on their approach to their work, their preferred style of working and a sense of how they can complement each other. The discomfort can come from the fact that, as their exploration of each other enters a deeper phase, they may well uncover aspects of each others' way of working or interpersonal issues arising between them which need to be raised and addressed. There is often an awareness that some friction is an inevitable part of developing a successful co-facilitative relationship. This was recognized by one co-facilitator during our research:

> 'When you're working with somebody who is strong, able to articulate what they want, knows what their agenda... is, and able to stand for their own boundaries, then you're going to get friction, and the best relationships I've had are when that friction develops into the ability to sort it out. Both of you have conflict solving skills.'

A potential danger at this stage is that co-facilitators can start to take their relationship and their ability to work together for granted, assuming that it will continue to work well for them. Co-facilitators involved in our research described the need for continued regular exchanges even within established pairings and the adverse impact that was likely to follow if such exchanges did not take place. Several people pointed out that if issues were left unresolved then the co-facilitative relationship could itself become a distraction from focusing on the dynamics within the client group, thus further reducing its effectiveness.

REFLECTION

▶ What difficulties have you encountered when co-facilitating with someone whom you know reasonably well?

▶ How easy/difficult have you found it to raise and deal with these issues?

▶ What sort of responses have you met with from the co-facilitators involved?

▶ Would you choose to handle these situations differently in future? If so, how?

One important way in which co-facilitators can progress effectively through this stage is by using their working relationship as a vehicle for their mutual learning. This can be achieved by focusing their regular work reviews and exchanges of feedback on specific learning goals which they have identified for themselves. This learning orientation helps co-facilitators to be honest and open in the giving and receiving of feedback since, rather than feeling defensive about their behaviours and actions, they have already identified a willingness to explore – and possibly change – them. Each co-facilitator therefore takes responsibility for their own development and for supporting the development of their colleague(s), in a way which mirrors the learning process which they hope to encourage and enable within the client group. These learning goals can relate to co-facilitators' personal and professional development, thus capturing one of the major benefits of co-facilitation as described in Chapter 2. The goals set also give another clear purpose and provide an additional framework for the regular reviews undertaken, which further increases their value.

REFLECTION

► Have you consciously used co-facilitation as an
opportunity for furthering your own and your
colleagues' learning?

► How could you improve the way in which you use
co-facilitation as a learning vehicle in future?

► What learning goals could you set for yourself?

► How could you most effectively support your
co-facilitators in their learning as you work together?

In addition to this emphasis on learning, co-facilitators at this stage of
their relationship will be refining the way in which they work together
to achieve the intended outcomes of particular work projects. This
improvement will require more detailed exploration of the individual
and interpersonal issues arising within the client group, analysis of their
impact on the learning process, and discussion of the interventions likely
to be most effective in enabling maximum group and individual development. Co-facilitators are increasingly likely to experiment and take
risks in trying out new ways of helping groups to move forward towards
their desired goals, as they feel confident in their own skill level and supported by their co-facilitator in pushing out the boundaries of their facilitation.

REFLECTION

▶ Have you noticed any differences between reviews held by you in newly formed relationships compared with more familiar co-facilitator relationships?

▶ How has your analysis of the work you are doing differed?

▶ How would you like your reviews to develop in future?

As before, there is no set duration for this stage of development. Some co-facilitators will progress quite quickly through this stage, while others may never progress beyond it – either their working relationship will get stuck at this level of development or they may decide to terminate the relationship due to a lack of real satisfaction with how it is developing. What is clear is that progress through this stage can be aided by taking positive action to improve your co-facilitation. This may involve making simple arrangements to stay in touch in between periods of working together, as well as by using more direct methods. Some guidelines regarding possible ways of achieving this progress are given in Chapter 6.

Below we outline two case studies which we hope will help you to recognize when your co-facilitative relationships are in this stage of development, and to start considering how you might get most benefit from this stage.

—————————————— **CASE STUDY 1** ——————————————

Juliet and Sean had co-facilitated together on a number of occasions over a period of two years. They typically felt that they worked well together and they achieved very positive results with their client groups. However, while co-facilitating a workshop for senior line managers within a retail company which was designed to support the move to a new business culture, they experienced some difficulty. Juliet perceived Sean as dominating the group, by positioning his chair directly at the front of the group. She felt physically side-lined – literally! She also thought that he made overly lengthy interventions, which left her feeling as though she was taking a minor role and making a lesser contribution to the group. This impression of his domination was further increased as Sean made his interventions in a loud voice.

From his perspective, Sean felt that Juliet always had to add to what he said, as though improving on it. If he introduced an activity, she would provide extra clarification for the group as to its purpose or its process. Sean started to feel that Juliet was competing with him and he felt resentful of her contributions. He began to feel competitive too.

REFLECTION

1. What do you see as the key issues between Juliet and Sean?
2. What do you think that Sean and Juliet could do to resolve their difficulties?
3. What do you think the effect would be if they were unable to discuss or resolve them:
   ▶ on their co-facilitation;
   ▶ on the work being undertaken?
4. How would you resolve similar difficulties when co-facilitating?
5. What have you learnt from this review?

—————————————— **CASE STUDY 2** ——————————————

Suzanne and Harriet were in the middle of co-facilitating an 18-month programme for internal trainers and developers, which they had designed together. They were used to working together periodically and had done so over a period of several years. They both felt that they shared some core beliefs about development and the role of the facilitator in enabling individual and group learning.

During one residential part of the programme they were exploring group dynamics and the role of the facilitator, using the participants themselves as a vehicle for examining these issues. There were a number of tensions within the group, which the residential part was starting to help them to surface and address. During one session, led by Suzanne, a difference in the time required for exploring a particular issue arose between two subgroups. Suzanne significantly over-ran the time allotted to the session, though Harriet and other group members in the second subgroup clearly signalled that they had no energy or interest left for this particular exploration. Harriet was additionally concerned that the next session, which she was going to lead, was going to be significantly reduced in time due to other constraints.

The session was designed to provide the group with an in-depth opportunity to exchange feedback, something which she felt they needed to do in order to surface their tensions and move forward as individuals and collectively. Harriet felt angry that her comments and those of her subgroup had been ignored by Suzanne, but she had not wanted to enter into an argument in front of the group so they had waited until Suzanne's group was ready. As a result, the feedback session was curtailed, although it proved to be a very powerful experience for the group.

REFLECTION

1. How would you describe the source of Suzanne and Harriet's difficulty?
2. In Harriet's situation, what would you have done:

   ▶ within the group session;
   ▶ afterwards, in reviewing your co-facilitation?

3. What have you learnt from this case study which you could apply to your own co-facilitation?

These case studies describe relationships which we define as functioning at the developing stage: they are reasonably mature and successful, but there is still some lack of awareness of the more difficult issues arising between the co-facilitators and some reluctance to deal with them. The movement into the third stage of co-facilitative relationships is characterized by a qualitative change in the depth of the exploration of personal, interpersonal and work issues, and by the ability to recognize and deal effectively with more complex and challenging issues. Again, it is difficult to describe exactly where the boundary lies, but it can be identified and experienced by those concerned. The transition is accompanied by high levels of confidence on the part of both (all) co-facilitators in their ability to resolve potentially difficult issues.

The partnership stage

At this stage the co-facilitative relationship is a mature one, in terms of how the co-facilitators are working together rather than the actual duration of their relationship. However, the development of the relationship to this high level of effectiveness does require time and attention, as one co-facilitator highlighted: 'I would want here to emphasize that my best co-facilitation relationships have developed over months and years rather than days and weeks.'

The partnership stage is informed by the development which the co-facilitators have already experienced together, particularly by the high levels of skill in reviewing their work and exchanging feedback which they have acquired during the previous phase. The partnership stage is marked by high levels of trust, support and challenge, enabling the recognition and confronting of issues which more typically form the hidden agenda in co-facilitative relationships – such as, for example, significant issues of projection and transference, and primal issues of sexuality, gender and identity. There is a mutual ability to be aware of issues as they arise, to acknowledge them and to work them through. The co-facilitators are accepting of the fact that issues will emerge and see the exploration of these as opportunities for their learning, rather than as problems to be overcome. Both (all) co-facilitators at this stage are able to acknowledge the 'darker' and primal aspects of themselves, such as competitiveness, the need for power and sexuality, which again supports the exploration of any issues arising. Co-facilitators may also explore the meaning of their philosophy and values again, but in a much more personal way than previously. As co-facilitators have a deep understanding of each other and themselves, their interaction moves into these deeper levels of experiential reality as defined by Barber (1994). Figure 5.2 shows the relationship between the depth of the co-facilitator interaction and their opportunities for learning.

The partnership stage is characterized by high learning as co-facilitators test and extend their personal boundaries and those of their relationship, in order to achieve ever greater degrees of success in their work. Their learning, and that of the groups they work with, is likely to be deep and significant. There is no identifiable end point to this stage of development. Co-facilitators may continue to develop both personally and professionally by working together, or they may decide to look for fresh sources of challenge if they feel that their opportunities for learning together are beginning to diminish.

The partnership stage represents the closest and most successful working relationship between co-facilitators, where each recognizes that they provide complementary skills and attributes of equal value to their clients and themselves. This does not mean that their contributions will always be equal, but that over time their input will be of similar value and acknowledged as such. The term 'partnership' captures the spirit of co-operation, participation, collaboration, teamwork and sharing which defines this stage of co-facilitation. The following descriptions of being in a co-facilitative relationship at this stage of development, taken from co-facilitators who were involved in our research, highlight the intensity of the experience, both for the co-facilitators themselves and for the groups with whom they work.

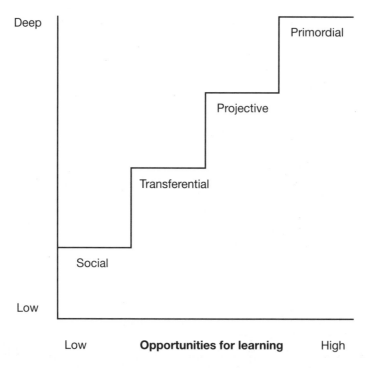

Figure 5.2 Levels of co-facilitator interaction

'A very high level of openness and honesty… in terms of where we were with things, where we were at with each other, when we were pissing each other off, when we were really enjoying each other's company, when we felt the session could have done with something else…'

'The learning was far, way beyond what we normally learn… much more primeval and deep… the effect that had on me was to bring things into very sharp relief, help me reflect a lot on myself, on me in this particular period of my life, discover a lot about myself, the effect I can have on others and that others can have on me… in a very tangible way.'

'A time in our relationship when we had cleared many difficult issues including those around sexuality so we each felt very clear to simply delight in each other. From our own feelings and feedback from the group we were fun to be with, light and deep, seamless, uncompetitive, fun and funny, loving, supportive and very challenging.'

We hope that these descriptions will help you to recognize when you are in a co-facilitative relationship which is functioning at this high level of effectiveness. Some of the key aspects of the partnership stage, which may also help you to differentiate it from the developing stage and to work towards it, are:

- very little cannot be discussed between you and your co-facilitator;
- the nature of some of the issues being explored;
- the depth of the exploration;
- the high level of trust, support and challenge experienced;
- the high level of risk taking with each other and with client groups;
- the intensity of the learning gained by all concerned;
- the feeling of being very 'in tune' with your co-facilitator;
- a deep self-knowledge and understanding of your co-facilitator.

Some of the signs that the value and effectiveness of this co-facilitative relationship may be waning are:

- you focus more attention on each other than on the client group;
- your reviews tend to focus on personal and interpersonal issues rather than on the work being carried out;
- you have a sense of covering the same ground with one another;
- you are not learning at the same high rate;
- you have become so similar in the way in which you work that you no longer provide real added value.

REFLECTIONS

► Have you ever, either directly or indirectly, experienced a co-facilitative relationship at this stage of development?

► What differentiated it from other co-facilitative relationships?

► What effect did it have on you?

► How could you better prepare yourself to co-facilitate at this level of development?

► What could you do to help your current/future co-facilitators to work with you at this level?

If you decide that your co-facilitative relationship has run its course, it is important to acknowledge this and to utilize your high levels of skill in ensuring that the ending reflects the value which you have gained from the relationship. It is also important to recognize that not all of your future co-facilitative relationships will operate at this stage of development and that it will take time if some of them are to function at this level. There will need to be investment in your new working relationships, using the learning and experience which you have gained from your previous partnership. Hopefully, you will become increasingly skilled at facilitating your own relationships through to this stage of development.

SUMMARY

In this chapter we have explored how you can make an informed choice concerning your co-facilitators and therefore gear your relationships for success from the outset. We have outlined the importance of effective co-facilitation before describing the three stages of development which co-facilitative relationships may go through. We have highlighted the fact that not all relationships will progress through every stage, due to the early termination of some (for whatever reason) and due to the relative ineffectiveness of others and the inability or lack of willingness of the co-facilitators involved to do anything about this. We hope that these descriptions of the different stages have encouraged you to reflect on your past experiences of co-facilitation and to identify the stages of development which you have achieved.

Being aware of where your relationships have been effective and where they have become stuck or worked less well is an important first step towards becoming a more effective co-facilitator. We also hope that you feel motivated to try and aim for the partnership stage in your co-facilitation, as you can see the potential benefits to be gained. The next chapter will provide you with some practical ideas on how to progress your co-facilitative relationships through the different stages, using the awareness which you have already gained.

6

Working with Co-facilitative Process

The activities and reflections described in Chapters 4 and 5 will greatly enhance the inner dynamics and development of your co-facilitative practice. However, the following are additional and general ways in which to develop your skills as a co-facilitator, and any relationship between you and another facilitator.

RAISING AWARENESS

Whatever the dynamic occurring, awareness is the first stage of managing the processes effectively. Awareness gives us choice and choice allows us to experiment with different ways of effectively managing the relationship. In turn experimentation allows us to find the way which meets our needs most effectively.

Which of the various levels of awareness do we need? First, awareness in hindsight is a useful start, being able to look back at your experiences, make sense of them and use them to learn from. This is, however, awareness on a *there and then* basis, that is, the awareness does not occur as the sensation or need emerges, but later. A more advanced level of awareness is awareness in the 'here and now'. This is awareness of feelings, thoughts and needs *at the time*, moment by moment, not just later or in hindsight. When our awareness is operating in the here and now we are aware of our needs and the processes going on between facilitators as they happen. We are therefore in a much better position to act on our awareness at the time rather than later saying 'I wish I had said…' or 'I wish had done…'.

ACTIVITY: PHENOMENOLOGICAL TRACKING

You can carry out this activity by yourself, but it will be very useful to do this with your co-facilitator. The aim of phenomenological tracking is to raise awareness and insight, and to help you to learn how to be more aware.

1. Put yourself in a place where you can pay attention to yourself.

2. Now pay attention to what you start to notice or what comes into your 'field' of awareness. As things come into your attention state what you are noticing out loud. (This is where your co-facilitator can help by periodically asking you 'What are you noticing?') Your awareness might be in the environment around you, it might be within yourself, or it might be the point at which you meet the environment.

3. Follow your senses and try not to restrict what is coming into your awareness, but let your awareness rise until you are aware of many different levels. These are likely to include:

   ▶ what you hear;

   ▶ what you see;

   ▶ what you are touching;

   ▶ what various parts of your body are feeling like;

   ▶ where you are comfortable and uncomfortable;

   ▶ what you are thinking;

   ▶ what you are feeling;

   ▶ what you are imagining;

▶ what you are remembering;

▶ what your intuition is telling you.

4. You will find that, as you do this, you will become much more aware, especially about what you need at that particular time. It is this raised level of awareness that will really inform your co-facilitative practice once you are able to do this naturally on an ongoing basis.

Awareness of self is of primary importance. Areas you should be aware of are thoughts, feelings, sensations (what is your body doing), intuition, daydreams, memories, assumptions, nonverbals, what is getting your attention and how you are stopping yourself being fully 'present'. All these will give you clues to your needs and how you want to work with your co-facilitator. They may also lead you to a greater understanding of how you are contributing to the dynamics between you and your co-facilitator.

Awareness is a main key to dealing not only with power positions, but also with any of the dynamics between co-facilitators. There are three main zones of awareness.

- *Zone 1.*   Awareness of self. Direct experience of feelings, emotions and physical sensations.
- *Zone 2.*   Representation of external/internal reality, including thinking, remembering, daydreaming, anticipating, planning.
- *Zone 3.*   Awareness of the world through the senses. Touch, taste, smell, sight, hearing.

We can be 'seduced' into spending a lot of our time in any one of these zones of awareness. The problem is that while we restrict ourselves to any one or two zones, we are not paying attention to the 'whole' of us and the dynamics between the co-facilitators, and between them and the group. While we are not aware of the whole of ourselves and the dynamics between co-facilitators, we are not likely to be wholly effective in dealing with the group and our co-facilitator.

OPENING UP THE PROCESS

One of the ways in which co-facilitators restrict their development as a pairing is by keeping the process hidden. We often come across co-facilitators who talk to us or others about their co-facilitative relationship, but have omitted to talk to their own co-facilitator about the issues (either positive or negative).

Whatever the reasons, the fact is that development happens at a greatly accelerated rate when both facilitators work on it together rather than independently. Some of the most effective advice to facilitators reviewing their practice is to 'say what they are thinking' or simply to 'state what they notice'. It is amazing how many experienced and skilled facilitators hold back from saying what they want because they are attempting to rationalize or make sense of what they notice. In this way information often gets lost or misinterpreted and so again we would remind you to 'say what you are thinking/feeling.'

Part of this process is holding reviews of your practice as a pairing: in what ways can you do this? Our guess is that you will be very familiar with one way of running reviews. This is often around the framework of 'What went well?' and 'What could we do differently and better?' In itself this is fine for a basic review structure, but some other questions you might like to ask are as follows.

- What do I/we do brilliantly?
- If I were to be the world's best facilitator, what else would I be doing?
- What was the content?
- What was the process?
- What is going on now during this review?
- What do you notice about me?
- Who am I like?
- How am I like you?
- How am I different from you?
- If I were you, what would it be like?
- What else can we do to be even better?
- What is happening to me right now?

Apart from using just words, try something different for your reviews, such as these ideas.

- *Metaphor.* If we were to describe our co-facilitative practice as a metaphor, what would it be? Now, talking around that metaphor, how do parts of this metaphor relate to our practice together?
- *Story.* Describe our co-facilitative practice as if you were telling a story. Here is your starter – 'Once upon a time…' What would be your ideal ending to this story?
- *Pictures.* Take some pens and a piece of flipchart paper each. Draw a picture that represents how you see our co-facilitative practice. When you have finished, share your drawings with each other and talk through their meaning to each other. What would you like to add to each picture?

PUTTING YOURSELF IN YOUR CO-FACILITATOR'S SHOES

In many approaches, there is reference to the ability to understand what it is like to be the other person. In co-facilitation, this is a very good way of understanding your partner and becoming aware of issues such as projections and transferences.

This does not just mean imagining what it must be like in your co-facilitator's position, but actually being able to be in their position including experiencing their thoughts and feelings. Seeing the other person's point of view is a phrase that is commonly used, but this is commonly done at a superficial level.

Some NLP (neuro-linguistic programming) practitioners use an approach called 'perceptual positions'. This involves 'stepping into' one of three positions.

- *First position* is when you are simply being 'you', seeing the other person through your own eyes and experiencing the world as you. In this position it is good to expand your own awareness of self as discussed above.
- *Second position* involves seeing the world through your co-facilitator's eyes, ears and senses, as well as understanding their feelings and thoughts. Becoming skilled at attaining this position will allow you closely to appreciate the other person's feelings, thoughts and senses. This in turn will enable you to understand their reaction to you and the co-facilitative relationship.
- *Third position* involves seeing the relationship and interactions of the facilitators from outside the relationship (this is sometimes referred to as the helicopter view). This can be particularly useful when you are unclear about what is going on in the relationship or when things seem difficult.

The perceptual positions approach is much more powerful when it is actually used, rather than just seen on paper. Try the following exercise.

ACTIVITY: PERCEPTUAL POSITIONS

1. Find a quiet place where you can concentrate for at least 30 minutes. Place three chairs in a triangle facing each other.

2. Label each chair – you, your co-facilitator, outsider.

3. Sit in the chair 'as you' (first position). Think about a specific interaction/discussion that you have had with your co-facilitator. Now put yourself back into the shoes of you during that interaction. Take your time to re-live the interaction. Pay attention to your thoughts, feelings, wants, fears, physical sensations and anything else which comes to the 'foreground' for you. What do you notice?

4. When you are ready stand up, after a minute or so prepare to sit in the chair of the other facilitator (second position). When you feel ready, sit in that chair, at the same time putting yourself in their place. Thinking of the same interaction/discussion, now pay attention to your thoughts, feelings, sensations, wants, fears and anything else which comes to the foreground. What do you notice?

5. When you are ready, stand up and prepare to become an independent observer to the interaction between the two facilitators. Again, when ready, sit in the chair of the 'observer' (third position) and look at the other two chairs as if the interaction is going on in front of you. What do you notice?

(NB If you are truly in the third position you are likely to be feeling less emotional and more objective to the interaction between the facilitators.)

WORKING AT A SYMBOLIC LEVEL

Many facilitators work mostly at a 'head' level, that is working with the conscious, logical and rational elements of our lives. However, there is another important level for us to operate on, which can be a powerful way of developing our co-facilitative relationships. This is working at a symbolic level.

Metaphor is one way of doing this, as we saw earlier. It will be helpful to you to find creative ways of accessing your co-facilitative development, by working at a symbolic level.

To do this successfully we often need to do it without trying to make sense of what we are doing and trust the process. It is important that we do not engage our sense-making ability until after the symbolic work is finished.

There follow some examples of working at a symbolic level.

Acting into

This is when one or both facilitators act into a part of themselves and/or the relationship that they are interested in exploring. It involves becoming the part of you that is the focus of your interest. So, for example, a facilitator who is exploring their tendency to go along with anything and everything that is said, may 'act into' disagreeing with everything in the conversation for a period of ten minutes. What will happen by doing this, is that as the facilitator acts into it, they will become more aware of their feelings, thoughts and beliefs around the issue.

If you wish to expand this method further, you can develop a whole play or drama which signifies the issue you are examining. Don't script it, just go with your instincts.

Using colours

The idea is to use colours as an unconscious metaphor for aspects of yourself and your relationships. To carry this exercise out you need to find something (we have used fabrics) with many colour choices. For example, you can use crayons or paints. Each of you picks two or three colours on instinct without thinking too much about it. Once you have done this you can then spend some time discussing how these colours represent you and your co-facilitative practice.

If you want to take this further, you can compare your colours and discuss how they might mix or clash, and what happens when these colours are mixed.

Making or sculpturing

For some people a powerful method of using symbols to aid understanding is by making things. You may use any material that you have – paper, plasticine or modelling clay. Again, try making something that you feel might represent you and/or the facilitative relationship. Review and process as with the exercise above.

Movement

Physical activity and freedom of expression can be very enlightening for many people. Although social conditioning often makes this difficult and embarrassing, if this is overcome, it is also powerful. This activity can be carried out in many ways including positioning yourself and your co-facilitator in a way that represents how you work together, using slow movement, through to dance.

Myths and legends

Tell the story of your co-facilitation as if it were a legendary tale, say in Medieval England or Ancient Greece. Review in terms of the key elements of the story and how that might relate to current practice. One further option is to create a story jointly.

Reviewing these types of exercise needs to be left until after the exercise, if you review at all. Often the act of carrying out such exercises can serve its purpose, and reviewing could reduce the impact, or not add anything new.

If you do decide to review, we suggest that you follow some of the processes described in Chapter 3, until you have developed some of your own procedures for reviewing.

DEVELOPING THE COMMUNICATION BETWEEN YOU

We have already discussed various aspects of the communication between co-facilitators (see levels of contact in Chapter 4). Each particular pairing will have its own repetitive pattern of communication, and its own strengths and weaknesses. To develop the communication, co-facilitators need to understand the patterns of communication as a whole. There are many excellent models of communication which can be useful in this analysis of your communication. For example, transactional analysis is one way of helping you understand the repetitive idiosyncrasies of your communication.

There are a number of elements that you may consider in your communication. You will be operating within your 'boundary', that is the levels within which we are used to operating and feel safe in operating. An excellent way of developing your communication is to push out this boundary and experiment with new methods. You are likely to know if you are pushing out the boundary by your own physical reaction. When you touch on something new there will be a physical reaction. Excitement, fear, resistance, anger and butterflies in the stomach, are just a few of the possible reactions facilitators can have to expanding boundaries. The following exercise will help you identify and expand these boundaries.

ACTIVITY

Stage 1 In the circle below, write down the topics that you and your co-facilitator usually talk about. Also describe here the way that you usually communicate (you might like to use the 'levels of contact' listed in Chapter 4 as a guide).

Stage 2 Outside the circle, write down the topics that you and your co-facilitator do not talk about. Also, write here the levels of communication that you do not communicate on.

Stage 3 From what is currently written down outside the circle, what could be moved to the edge of the circle or boundary? If you were to say something that was right at the boundary, what would it be?

Stage 4 How will you move those boundaries to include some of the things outside the circle?

This exercise leads on to an important consideration in your communication and that is to consider the question of what is *not* being said. In other words, what are you putting outside your boundary?

Feedback is a major way of improving your co-facilitative practice and therefore developing your feedback practice is key. We have found many ways that different co-facilitators structure their feedback. Below we describe one way which we believe to be effective.

One of the difficulties with offering feedback is that it is a rich ground for projections. Remember that we tend to see in others what is also present in ourselves, so the feedback given often says as much about the giver of the feedback as the receiver. If the feedback is useful, we need to try and be clear about what are projections from the giver and what are genuine observations. The following format will help you with this.

Feedback structure

1. *State what you notice/noticed.* Give direct observations, no interpretations and specific examples. This helps to stop projections and allows the receiver to obtain facts.
2. *Your interpretations/views on what you have noticed.* This allows the receiver to compare their own views of the observation with the giver of the feedback. It allows projections to be used positively and to be understood as projections.
3. *The effect/impact on you of what you noticed.* This allows the receiver to understand the possible impact of what they were observed doing. It gives them the choice of how to react.
4. *Suggestions for what to keep and what to change.* This gives the receiver some extra ideas and choices.

UNFINISHED BUSINESS

The term 'unfinished business' was coined in Gestalt psychology theory. This states that, usually, we all have the ability to get our physical and psychological needs met, and that there is a cycle to us getting our needs met. This cycle is called a Gestalt formation and, as one need is met, it falls away and is replaced by another emerging need. Figure 6.1 shows the Gestalt cycle.

Figure 6.1   The Gestalt cycle

We all have emotional and psychological needs which will emerge during our co-facilitative relationship, such as approval, love, recognition, companionship, stimulation, interest, acceptance and communication. When a need is not met it remains unsatisfied and disturbs the healthy pattern of emerging needs. That is, it becomes 'unfinished business' in that it does not just go away. The unfinished business, and other needs not met, remain with us and we become less clear and less ready for the next emerging need and experience.

Through this we all have ways in which we habitually stop our needs being met. Gestalt psychology refers to these as interruptions. For example, a facilitator notices that his co-facilitator talks to group members in a relaxed, informal way, frequently and freely. He also notices that the same co-facilitator talks to him in a more abrupt and formal way. His need for acceptance and friendship are not being met. Unaware that this reminds him very closely of what his mother did with him when he was a child, he does what he used to do then and withdraws from having much conversation with his co-facilitator. He also withdraws from much contact with the group and therefore feels that he is not liked by them. This in turn impedes him getting many other needs met from the group, and he becomes less ready and prepared for the next experience with this co-facilitator and the group as a whole.

Now, in your co-facilitative relationship, it is easy to build up this unfinished business and this will restrict the healthy development of your practice and relationship. Some easy feelings, thoughts and behaviours to look for as clues to unfinished business are, either feelings of dissatisfaction with or without knowing why this is so, or finding yourself thinking 'I wish I had said…', or behaving in a way with your facilitator that you know you do not want to, and yet still finding yourself doing it. Many of the exercises you have gone through in this book so far will help you in this respect. Another exercise for this goes as follows.

ACTIVITY: 'I WISH I HAD SAID...'

1. Sit opposite your co-facilitator.

2. Thinking of the times you have worked together, start by saying 'I wish I had said...' followed by 'What I want is...'.

3. Continue this exercise for at least three minutes. Don't think too much about what you are saying, but try to let the words flow out.

Note

Do not think about your answers too much, as this is where many people interrupt the process of saying and getting what they want. The more you can 'free flow' in this exercise, the more likely you are to get in touch with your needs.

SUMMARY

This chapter is aimed at helping the reader develop the co-facilitative relationships that they are in, by outlining a number of broad developmental processes that will develop the relationship. It contrasts with Chapters 3 and 4, which have outlined specific elements of the relationship. The aim here has been purely and broadly to develop.

It has covered development processes including:

- *awareness* – raising the conscious dynamics of you and your co-facilitator, and the relationship between you;
- *opening up the process* – making the implicit explicit so that it can be developed;
- *putting yourself in the co-facilitator's shoes* – learning to experience the relationship from the other person's point of view;
- *working at a symbolic level* – using different ways of accessing our developmental processes other than talking;
- *communication* – pushing out the boundaries of our communication;
- *unfinished business* – learning to get our needs met.

In the next chapter we will outline some of the choices that you have in terms of the kind of relationship that you may choose to have with your co-facilitator. It takes the reader through some case studies which highlight the differences in the relationships that each of the co-facilitators has chosen, and hence some of the choices open to you as a practising co-facilitator.

7

Different Co-facilitative Models

This chapter will be of practical use to you, whether you are in a co-facilitative relationship already or are about to enter into one. Its aim is to give you some alternative models for working as a co-facilitator. By reading this chapter you will be able to choose the type of relationship you wish to have with your co-facilitator. We would add a note of caution to this, which is that no relationship is static, so it is important to review the type of relationship you have and want on a regular basis.

TYPES OF RELATIONSHIP

Equality relationship

In the equality co-facilitative relationship, the aim is to provide as much balance as possible between the co-facilitators in all aspects of the work. In the areas of balance the co-facilitators choose to have, there will be differences according to the pairing, but common areas for balance are influence with the group, ownership of the design and, in the amount of sessions run, level of intervention.

In many ways the equality relationship is the hardest to achieve due to the natural inequalities and skills experience that we each have, and the fact that often the environment around us emphasizes these differences. An example is the internal trainer working with an external consultant, where external consultants are more valued than employees within the company.

There is often an unchallenged assumption that equality should be the aim of all co-facilitative relationships. We would challenge this. Fitting the right relationship to the situation is a much more productive way of running your co-facilitation. Equality is only one of those options.

CASE STUDY I

William is a trainer working for a large, blue-chip company. He has eight years' experience of management development and training. He has been working on a project to implement self-managed work teams in one of his client areas. The project is at a stage where a number of teams are ready to be trained.

William prefers to facilitate and train with another facilitator, and the intensity of the programme will need two trainers. With this in mind he asks an external consultant, Hannah, to run the events with him. She has experience of running these types of events with other companies.

First meeting

As the two already know each other, this meeting is spent with William explaining the work to Hannah as he sees it, and discussing the overall aim and outcomes for the work. At this point they also discuss what their own hopes, desired outcomes and fears for the work are.

They agree that it might be a good idea for Hannah to meet the client, and so she will carry out the needs identification separately from William, and that then they would meet to compare analyses. They also think that it might be good for Hannah to do this so that she could establish a relationship with the client, as William already had done so. They agree that at the next meeting they will contract how they will work together, compare diagnosis of the identified needs and co-design the event.

Second meeting

They share their diagnosis of the needs identified and find that although they are generally the same, there are some differences. After discussing the differences they decide to follow one particular route for each difference and review after the first event whether or not this was the correct decision, and what might need to change. They agree, however, on the core issues and what must be achieved above all else. The organization has its own methods for evaluation of programmes against desired outcomes, which both facilitators agree is a suitable method in this case. William agrees to take responsibility for ensuring this happens and agrees to meet with Hannah to discuss the results when it has happened. They agree a date to do this.

At this point they decide it might be a good idea to agree how they will work together. The 'contract' that they agree consists of the following elements:

1. They will play an equal role in the work, but will try to utilize the strengths that they each have. William is an experienced trainer, especially in the use of exercises as a vehicle for learning. He also has an in-depth knowledge of the company and the work of this particular team. Hannah is a skilled facilitator of groups, especially in attitude change situations. She also has much experience of the implementation of self-directed work team cultures across different companies.

2. The roles in the event will follow these strengths, although they also agree that according to the group during the event, they will review and change their roles accordingly. They will aim to play an equal role in the event and work with those individuals who seem to respond to each of them.

3. William will liaise with the client over arrangements for the training, but if they need to meet the client or the client's team, then they will do this jointly.

4. They will review at lunchtime and in the evenings of each day on the programme. The reviews will be constrained to 15 minutes each. Each person can use this to review whichever aspects of the programme or working together that they wish. At the end of the work they will meet for one hour to review the whole piece of work.

5. In terms of groundrules, Hannah would like to be able to run over time on her sessions if the session warrants it, and would like William to chip in wherever he likes while paying attention to the group process and direction that Hannah is taking. She would like to be able to sit out one of William's sessions if she is tired or needs to think about her next session. William agreed and added for himself that he would like them to review regularly whether or not what they are doing is meeting the identified aims for the programme. He does not want to be interrupted in his sessions as it would prevent him concentrating fully. He says that his pet hate is being corrected by his co-facilitator in front of the group.

6. Hannah states that the feedback that she would like would be on:
   - her challenging of the group and individuals;
   - how clear the theory inputs that she gives are;
   - her relationship with the group generally;
   - her presence and energy.

   William states that he would like feedback on:
   - his tendency to focus on one or two individuals in the group;
   - how engaged or withdrawn he seems with the group;
   - his non-verbal messages.

7. They agree that they will design together in broad outline now and that they will each take away certain sessions to flesh out more. They will send each other their work and finalize the design over the phone/fax etc.

Hannah's strength is in establishing the broad outline of the design, whereas William is good at the detail. They start by discussing their approaches to learning and how they would translate that into a design bearing in mind the agreed diagnosis. William prefers to use outdoor activities and reviews as a vehicle for learning, while Hannah likes to use day-to-day work-based issues as a vehicle for learning. Both agree that using the group process as it arises is an effective way of facilitating learning. They agree on an approach to learning that will suit this situation, using exercises and reviews based on workplace issues, followed by practical work placed action planning. William agrees to ask his training administrator to carry out the booking of venue and the joining letters for delegates. They agree that Hannah will be copied in on all correspondence.

REFLECTION

▶ In the above example, what are the key indicators that the aim is to develop an equal co-facilitative relationship?

▶ What else could William and Hannah do to establish balance in the relationship?

▶ Having read the above example, what would you see as the advantages and disadvantages of this type of co-facilitative relationship?

Key points

There are a number of key points to be noted from the above example. Note that William in this case *chose* Hannah to work with. We do not know exactly why he chose her, other than the fact that she has some experience in the type of work. At this point there will already be numbers of projections at work. For example, William already has some views on how Hannah will be in the work. As he chose her, we can assume that they are probably positive projections, which may be accurate or not. The danger is that Hannah may not live out these projections or even be aware of them until they share expectations of each other. In this case, even before they have met, there is a potential for problems and disappointment unless they become aware of and work with the projections. Choices over whom to work with are often based around projective influences.

There is already an irony here and it is an important point. This is that they are *not* equal. William has more experience with this company and Hannah has more facilitative experience. Therefore absolute equality will not be achieved. The aim is to achieve a balance rather than total equality. The discussion as to what each facilitator considers to be equality may be a useful conversation. In this case they seem to view equality as client contact, equal amount of group time and joint responsibility for the work.

They recognize that they each have strengths and hence have worked toward those strengths. This is a positive step. We find that facilitators often interpret equality as acting as if both facilitators are equally skilled in all aspects of the work. In reality of course, this is never so.

Their design seems to be a half-way house between each of their preferred methods, the hope being that it will utilize the best of both approaches. However, it may negate the positive aspects of both approaches. It is therefore an experiment. This is a good example of how the co-facilitative relationship has a direct impact on the work itself and how it is carried out.

Within the facilitation, groups will tend to notice differences in the co-facilitators and aspects of the relationship between them. Each will have their own transferences and projections towards each facilitator; how you facilitate will either encourage or dispel these. If you can use them and work with them, then all the better. For example we have often worked in situations where one of us is considered 'friendly' and the other to be more 'detached'. We have used this to play a role of 'supportive facilitator' and 'challenging facilitator'. Sometimes we have then swapped roles. This can be a very useful way of starting to work on transferences and always opens up the group process!

The main benefits of this model of co-facilitation are as follows. Facilitators can switch roles reasonably easily and this gives them greater flexibility in the work. This model of co-facilitation seems to achieve joint ownership more easily, if it is carried out well. This is probably partly because of the importance of each facilitator in their respective roles and the motivation that this brings with it. This approach allows joint development and for each facilitator to work on their particular development needs.

The group can easily relate to either facilitator, rather than seeing one as the 'senior' facilitator. In turn this means that it allows either facilitator to work with individual's issues on the programme, according to who is approached by the group member.

However, this is the most difficult type of relationship to achieve well, due to the balance needed. It is easy for the facilitators to fall into a less balanced role, habitually, or as result of being treated as such by the group members. Because of the balance aimed for in this relationship, it tends to be one of the most time-consuming ways of co-facilitating, with a lot of time invested before the group work is carried out. The type of relationship will vary according to the people involved, the work itself and the group involved. It is therefore very difficult to transfer one experience across to another co-facilitative relationship; each co-facilitative relationship needs to be approached freshly.

Learner–coach facilitation

This type of co-facilitative relationship is where one facilitator takes the role of learner and the other acts as coach to the learner. Within this there are a number of possible roles for either person. The learner can take a participation role or an observing role, or any combination of the two, while the coach can also act as an observer, giving feedback and coaching to the other facilitator, or act as a fully participating facilitator. The aim of this type of relationship is to develop the facilitator during the course of the work. It aims to recognize that one facilitator is more experienced or knowledgeable than the other for this particular piece of work. To work successfully the development need must be clearly identified, and it is very important that the roles within the relationship are also clearly identified and agreed.

CASE STUDY 2

Mervyn and Helen are employed to facilitate counselling skills programmes. Mervyn is a professional counsellor and trainer; Helen is new to her training role, although she has had some group training experience in the past. They have some experience of working together, as Helen was a delegate on some of Mervyn's training two years ago. She sees herself as being in a trainee period in her career and has set herself the target of being able to run these programmes herself in one year, although she does not feel confident or experienced enough to do so currently. She sees Mervyn playing a key part in her development and would like him to be her coach.

First meeting (contracting)

They contract to operate with Mervyn being the lead trainer and Helen being the trainee. The question they address here is to see what this means in practice.

Helen sees her role as still being a tutor and even running as much of the training (in terms of time or sessions run) as Mervyn. She sees that the role of Mervyn is to own the programme in the sense of being the decision maker about how it is run and who does what.

The requests she makes of Mervyn are to lead the programme, to agree to spend up to an hour each day with her as a coach and to deal with the more difficult or in-depth sessions that are involved in the programmes.

Mervyn sees his role being to run the programme. His expectations are to run all the sessions initially and maybe for Helen gradually to facilitate more sessions in subsequent programmes. His reservations are around the fact that what Helen is suggesting will distract his attention away from the programme, giving him a dual and possibly conflicting role. He also has reservations about what Helen is suggesting, as it seems to indicate that she wants to become a 'copy' of himself and replicate the way that he chooses to run the programme. He is comfortable with the idea of being Helen's coach and in eventually co-facilitating with her. Mervyn's hopes for the programme are focused on the outcomes for the delegates, but he states his apprehension about having a second facilitator and how this is going to work.

Having discussed the different views on this they agree that for the first programme Helen will have a 'watching' brief, after which they will discuss the programme, its content and the way Mervyn runs it. This discussion will lead into a joint redesign where Mervyn will still have the lead facilitator role, but Helen will have more of an active part as time goes on. For the subsequent programmes they will devote half-an-hour each day of the programme to coaching for Helen, in terms of developing her own style of facilitation in this programme.

The feedback and development coaching that Helen agrees with Mervyn for herself, includes discussing and learning the content of the programme, development of her counselling skills, and feedback regarding her facilitation skills and style.

Mervyn asks for feedback about the design of the programme in practice and whether it meets the needs of the delegates. The groundrules they discuss include an agreement about the first programme being run by Mervyn, where Helen is an observer and the groundrules are built around this. Due to the evolving nature of the contract and relationship, they agree to redefine the groundrules each time that they start a new programme.

Key points

This agreement obviously has consequences for the normal contractual issues (see Chapter 3). Initially the decisions regarding preparation, design and so on, will be carried out by Mervyn, but as the coaching agreement progresses, this is likely to change and develop. Therefore, in this case the contract is very much a live contract that is constantly reviewed, improved and updated. The one element of the contract that is likely to remain the same for the first year is the relationship of coach to learner. How this manifests itself in practice will, however, evolve with the work and the relationship.

The most obvious positive use of this model is as a structured learning and coaching method. In this sense it can be used as development for a facilitator in a particular topic, programme or as a personal development programme. It is a very good way for a facilitator to gain live experience, without jeopardizing a programme. Delegates tend to be very clear about the respective role of each facilitator, so their expectations of each facilitator are also clear. Because of the clear agreed roles of each, it makes further decisions (such as design) easier to make.

It is important, however, that this does not become a static relationship. We have come across co-facilitators who have been working on the same programme together as coach and learner for three years. Clearly there comes a time when the co-facilitative roles are taken out of habit rather than out of conscious choice. It is imperative therefore that this type of relationship is a constantly evolving one which is regularly reviewed. The main aim of this type of co-facilitative relationship needs to be learning for the facilitator in this role. It can attract a lot of transferential and projective material, especially that of 'good and bad facilitator'. Delegates can often dismiss the facilitator in the learning role and, in turn, if the learner facilitator runs a session they can find it more difficult to gain credibility. This dynamic can therefore directly impact on the learning for delegates.

Team facilitation

We were recently involved in a programme which had four facilitators in total and this set us thinking about the co-facilitative relationship where more than two people are involved. What particular implications does this have and what are the best ways to deal with this?

It seems that it can work in a number of ways. Some facilitators prefer all of the facilitators to attend each session run. However, the extra choice that team facilitation allows is for some of the facilitative team to leave for some sessions, and there still to be two facilitators facilitating the session. Our experience is varied in this respect, and either can work, but both need to be very clearly contracted for.

―――――――――――――― CASE STUDY 3 ――――――――――――――

Daniel was a training manager for a large company and was asked to project lead a modular, year-long senior management programme. One of the modules was an advanced personal development and interpersonal skills module. He decided to put together a team of facilitators to run this module for a number of reasons. While he had been a facilitator of groups in the past, his more recent duties had not involved him in groupwork, so he felt 'rusty' and had not run this module before. He had been with the group throughout the training as the organizer of the programme and had an in-depth knowledge of the development issues for each delegate. Throughout this time he had built up a good rapport with the group. He enlisted the help of Darren, who was the only facilitator in the company who had run this module before, Adrian who was an external consultant with a specialism in interpersonal skills and Sue, an experienced company trainer, who may be asked to run this programme next time.

The programme was a high profile one in the company and considered essential to the development of the management, so having four facilitators was considered a worthwhile investment of time and resources. Various of the four have worked together in pairs, but never as a four and some of them have never worked together.

First meeting

The four meet and look at the design of the programme from the last time it was run. From the evaluation and validation, they decide that the basic programme is good, but that whereas before it was run in a structured way, with timetabled sessions, this time they would respond to delegates' needs by running sessions according to needs as they arose. They agree the possible sessions in the programme and move on to contracting with each other.

The contracting involves the following points.

1. *Who will prepare what.* After the original meeting, they agree to prepare sessions according to strengths and interests.
2. *Who will carry out which session.*

3. *How they will decide who will 'work with' which delegate.*
4. *Who will 'sit in' on the others' sessions.* They agree that they need two facilitators for each session. The other facilitators have a choice about whether or not to sit in, but would play no part in the facilitation. This was apart from the third day, when each facilitator would be working with a small group.
5. *How they will co-facilitate when they run a session together.*
6. *What involvement the person(s) 'sitting in' will have for each session.*
7. *What each facilitator wants for themselves out of this programme.*
8. *What each facilitator sees as their strengths in relation to this programme, leading into agreeing the different roles of each of the facilitators.* They agree the following roles:

   • Daniel   organizer, some tutoring and facilitation, link to other modules, link to organizational issues, small groupwork;
   • Darren   main tutor and facilitator in terms of number of sessions, small groupwork, link and reference to how it was run last time;
   • Adrian   main tutor and facilitator, adding expertise in terms of design work and new approaches to interpersonal skills;
   • Sue   tutor and small group facilitator, leading the feedback to the facilitator group about their team process.

9. *When and how feedback will be given.*
10. *What feedback each of the facilitators wants from each other.*
11. *When during and after the programme they would review their working together.* They agreed to have a half-hour meeting each lunchtime to review that morning and plan for the afternoon. Each evening they agree to met for one-and-a-half hours, to review, give feedback and plan the next day. After this meeting each facilitator could then carry out their individual preparation.

In practice any issues which arose were around the relationships between them rather than the work itself. Darren and Adrian had worked together many times, as had Sue and Darren. In practice Daniel felt very much omitted from the group, as many of the conversations among the others did not include him or were carried out when he was doing some organizing duties. It was really a team dynamic of which all where unaware until Daniel mentioned it at a review. As a result, the facilitators added to their contract that they would only review and make decisions about the programme when all four were present. They also realized that the team dynamic was an important one which could have a direct impact on the running of the programme and so would be included in their reviews. They also realized from this that they had not agreed a very clear decision making process between them and decided that for subsequent programmes it would be useful to have one of them act as a 'lead facilitator', who would lead this group in terms of making decisions about the programme as it was being run.

Darren became aware during the programme that the other facilitators were looking to him to make all the decisions during the programme and to 'lead' the team of facilitators. He was uncomfortable with this as first it had not been contracted for as part of his role and, secondly, because this dynamic was one which 'happened' to him frequently, and he had been working on this as an issue for himself. This again was brought to awareness during one of the tutor reviews and worked on by the facilitators from this point onwards.

Key points

Having four facilitators/team facilitation tends to encourage many new dynamics. The possible projections and transferential material are quadrupled as there are now many different possible 'hosts' for each person's projections. As well as the projective and transferential issues associated with working in pairs, you also now have the dynamics of team working. In our experience this can often include the dynamics of inclusion/exclusion, decision making processes, pairing, emergence of a leader, communication issues, fight/flight and dependence, among many possible others.

These can be drawbacks to the co-facilitative process and the work. They need to be raised to awareness and worked on with the involvement of all the facilitators. Because there are more facilitators, this can obviously take more time and is often more difficult to deal with. Consensus decisions are often harder to reach for the same reasons. For the group the establishment of relationships with facilitators tends to be more fragmented, and this can lead to a 'them and us' relationship between facilitators and delegates, if it is not dealt with. The delegates might become confused about the respective roles of each facilitator and in this sense it might be difficult for all facilitators to build good rapport with the group. In terms of the projective influences from the group on to the facilitators, there is a greater chance of comparisons made by the delegates about the facilitators.

However, having a team of facilitators allows 'expertise' to be utilized fully. The ability to respond to delegates' needs quickly and accurately is enhanced, as is the flexibility of the facilitative team. Decisions, although harder to make, are often of greater quality if the facilitation team process is good. There will be a greater variety of views and opinions in terms of group process and the programme, and consequently the generation of more ideas. The 'bank' of knowledge is likely to be greater. The number of facilitators available means that you can afford to have someone there in a trainee facilitator capacity (as in the above example), either for learning for them or for learning about the programme. The availability of a team of facilitators allows for a greater amount and variety of support. In this sense also there are fewer demands on each individual facilitator in terms of time, which means that each facilitator will have more chance for reflection and observation. It can also mean that each facilitator has more energy and is less likely to experience facilitator burn-out.

SUMMARY

This chapter has outlined three possible models or types of co-facilitative relationships, which in our experience are the three most common forms found. These are:

- a co-facilitative relationship based on equality and balance;
- a co-facilitative relationship based on learner and coach roles;
- a co-facilitative relationship based on team facilitation.

There are many variations on each of these and probably many more types of co-facilitative relationship. This chapter has also outlined some of the issues and areas to be addressed in each of these types of co-facilitative relationship, based on some examples of them in practice.

8

Groups and Co-facilitators

Although the context in which co-facilitation occurs, that is working with groups engaged in progressing their own learning, has been implicit throughout this book, our main focus of attention has been on the relationship between the co-facilitators because of the influence we believe this exerts on the effectiveness of their work. However, we have no desire to encourage co-facilitators in developing an insular focus on their relationship to the detriment of their work with groups – which could be one, albeit misguided, response to our putting the spotlight on to this relationship for the first time. It is now timely, therefore, to focus our attention specifically on the interaction between co-facilitators and the groups with whom they work, and to explore some of the main dynamics of this relationship.

You might find it useful at this stage to turn back to Chapter 2, where the major advantages and difficulties of co-facilitating were described. Many of these descriptions focus on the potential effect of co-facilitation on the groups being worked with and we shall explore some of these in greater depth in this chapter.

We want to keep focused on the group's perspective of co-facilitation and of the co-facilitators themselves here. We have invited you to wear one set of glasses throughout this book and to use these to look in detail at the relationship between co-facilitators. Now, we are asking you to put on a different set of glasses for the purpose of gaining a new and different perspective on some of the issues which we have been discussing. We hope this adds to your learning about co-facilitation and encourages you to reflect on how effective your own practice has been, when seen from this perspective.

ANALYSIS OF CO-FACILITATOR/GROUP INTERACTIONS

If we want to be able to understand the relationship between co-facilitators and the groups with whom they work, we need to be able to analyse this. Without sound analysis we cannot assess the quality of the relationship, whether it is functioning as effectively as we should like, whether it is appropriate for the particular purpose of our work with a specific group, whether we want to change it and where we might most appropriately make those changes. We need this type of information before we can identify how we might go ahead in initiating any desired changes. In other words, we need to have a way of analysing whether our approach and methods are supporting our intended strategy or are limiting our effectiveness in achieving our purpose.

So, how can we undertake such analysis? We need to find ways of engaging in action research – that is, researching while we are actively pursuing our role as co-facilitators. In this way, analysis does not present us with additional workload or require that group members engage in giving us feedback of a sort which may sometimes lie outside their experience and/or capability. However, it does allow us to respond quickly and flexibly to whatever emerges as a result of our analysis.

The following represent some of the most useful (and therefore most used) ways in which we and other co-facilitators undertake this analysis. They are essentially very practical methods as, by its nature, action research demands approaches which can easily be integrated into normal everyday working activity. We shall explore how this information can be used later in this chapter.

Eye contact

We are very aware of the degree and nature of eye contact between ourselves as co-facilitators, and the individual group members with whom we are working. We have found that where co-facilitators have established good relationships with group members, then there is likely to be a high and regular amount of eye contact between them. They, as individuals, are attended to and one expression of this is the level of eye contact they receive from group members. Conversely, we have found that where one co-facilitator has failed to establish their individual credibility in this role with the group, then there tends to be significantly reduced levels of eye contact from the group to that person. The group or individual members within it are paying that co-facilitator minimum attention and, in doing so, one external (and therefore easily observable) manifestation of this is a withdrawal or reduction of direct eye contact. Of course, individuals within the group may give markedly differing levels of eye contact to the same facilitator, indicating that they have established relationships at quite different levels of effectiveness with different group members. There can, of course, also be differences between one group member's level of eye contact with different co-facilitators, indicating that they have developed a better relationship with a particular co-facilitator rather than their colleague or that their attention is focused on one particular co-facilitator for some reason.

By monitoring such differences in eye contact between group members and themselves, co-facilitators are given one indication of the way in which they are perceived collectively and individually, both by the group in general and by particular members within it. This information is easily noted throughout the period of working with a group and any marked shifts in the pattern of eye contact can be recognized. Of course, an interpretation has to be made of the level of eye contact and of any changes to this in order for this information to be utilized to improve the co-facilitation of that group. However, this can be done by discussion between the co-facilitators in a review meeting, using other data to support or counteract the initial interpretation being placed upon the level and type of eye contact.

REFLECTION

▶ Think back to one particular experience of co-facilitation. Were you aware of the level and type of eye contact which you received as co-facilitator? How would you describe it?

▶ Did you notice the eye contact your co-facilitator(s) got? Did it vary from yours in any way?

▶ What interpretation (if any) did you put on that?

▶ Did you discuss this with your co-facilitator? Together, what interpretation did you put on this data?

▶ Did you make any adjustments to your co-facilitation as a result?

▶ Consider your experience as a group member. Have you ever been conscious of giving a lot of eye contact to one particular co-facilitator? Why do you think this happened?

▶ Have you ever been conscious of not giving much eye contact to one particular co-facilitator? Why do you think you did this?

▶ What action (if any) might the different co-facilitators in these situations have taken to improve the effectiveness of their facilitation for you?

▶ How will you use your awareness of eye contact to enhance your co-facilitation in future?

Spoken exchanges

Another important way in which co-facilitators can analyse their relationship with both groups and individual group members is by monitoring the flow of verbal interactions between them. This technique is particularly useful in identifying the level of interaction between each co-facilitator and specific group members. It can then highlight whether there are any communication gaps where there has been little or no direct communication between one co-facilitator and one or more group members. Figure 8.1 gives an example of the way in which this can be done and of the resulting picture.

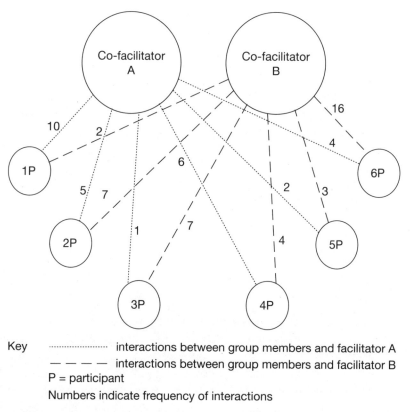

Key   ·············· interactions between group members and facilitator A

— — — — interactions between group members and facilitator B

P = participant

Numbers indicate frequency of interactions

Figure 8.1   Interaction mapping

If you carry out this mapping at various stages throughout your co-facilitation with a group, then you can start to see whether any patterns emerge where, for example, there is a particularly high level of interaction or where there is little or no direct verbal communication. The map itself does not tell you how to interpret this information. For instance, high levels of interaction between a co-facilitator and one group member could be the result of a close, intense relationship; this could indicate a group member who is overly dependent on the co-facilitator and their views; or one who values the co-facilitator's contributions but who checks out their applicability to their own situation in a self-responsible manner; or it could be indicative of extreme dislike so that every comment from the co-facilitator provokes an antagonistic reaction; and so on. You and your co-facilitator(s) will need to decide how to make sense of the data, taking into account other available sources of information.

One note of caution regarding the analysis of the volume of interactions between co-facilitators and group members is that this type of mapping only reveals the quantity – and not the quality or effectiveness – of these interactions. It therefore provides only a very partial indicator of what is occurring between co-facilitators and group members. However, having acknowledged its limitations, we still find it valuable as one way of analysing the relationship between co-facilitators and groups. Reviewing a map like the one shown in Figure 8.1 above can also indicate simple ways in which the co-facilitators might start to change their way of working with the group, by varying the amount or direction of their interventions. We have found that this can be powerful as a means of preventing over-dependence on one facilitator by the group or individuals within it.

Informal contact

Another way of analysing the relationship between co-facilitators and group members is to pay attention to the informal interactions which occur outside the formal group sessions. These can be informative because group members are not subject to the same disciplines or norms which may guide and influence their behaviour while working in the more structured group sessions. Paying attention to these interactions can mean noting the form and direction of individual requests for extra support or guidance; it may mean noting which co-facilitator is requested to explore particular points or issues in greater depth; or it might simply be noticing which group members choose to spend social time with which co-facilitator. Again, this information is open to different interpretations and co-facilitators will need to put this together with other data in order for it to be useful in understanding relations between themselves and group members.

These are just some of the ways in which co-facilitators can analyse their relationships with groups. You may already use some other methods or you may like to consider new ways in which you could undertake similar action enquiry. It is important that you select several methods for gaining and analysing information or you are likely to develop a very partial view of your relationships with groups. It is also important to recognize that there is no one truth which represents the reality of any group. Each co-facilitator and group member will have a somewhat different perception of the events that occur within that group and of the relationships which exist within it.

Such analysis is useful in informing your co-facilitation. You may decide that the existing relationship between co-facilitators and the group is an appropriate one, and decide to maintain the status quo. Alternatively, having conducted some analysis, you may decide to attempt to change the nature of this relationship or to shift some aspect of it, such as the relationship between one co-facilitator and certain group members. In turn, this may help you to decide on the relevance of certain interventions. It can help to ensure that you are clear about the intentions of your co-facilitation, which Heron (1989) has identified as one of the key skills of effective facilitators.

PURPOSES OF CO-FACILITATION

However, no analysis is of real value if you are unclear about the purpose of your co-facilitation. The most effective co-facilitation is about being, behaving and intervening in ways which are appropriate given the particular objectives which you are aiming to help group members to achieve, and given the circumstances within which you are working towards this. We do not believe that there are simple solutions which are applicable to every group and each situation. Your reflections regarding what is appropriate will therefore be informed by the purpose of your co-facilitation.

Clearly, there are numerous specific purposes which you may be working to help group members achieve. Here we will focus our attention on those where co-facilitating, rather than facilitating, may be particularly helpful – from the group members' perspective.

Experimentation

In Chapter 2, we gave our understanding of the term facilitation and what it is typically trying to achieve. This emphasized learning, rather than teaching or training and, more particularly, experiential forms of learning. An important part of experiential learning is experimentation, by which we mean that individual group members and the group as an entity are encouraged and supported in actively trying out new ways of behaving, interacting, thinking and so on.

We believe that co-facilitation can further support experimentation. There are some very practical reasons for this. Firstly, by having more than one facilitator, there is greater flexibility to split the group into two or more subgroups to work on different issues, according to what is most relevant for different group members. At the same time, the presence of a source of skilled feedback is still available to both/all subgroups, to aid the process of learning from reflections upon the experimentation. If, as facilitators, your preference is to allow group members to identify their own most important needs and how to address them, then co-facilitating offers greater flexibility in responding to their self-assessment.

While co-facilitating can offer more in-depth feedback from different perspectives to group members, highlighting that there is no one right way of interpeting actions and behaviours, there is a potential danger that co-facilitators may deprive group members of the space and opportunity to make their own comments and draw their own conclusions in relation to different experiments.

REFLECTION

► How have co-facilitators you have experienced helped encourage you to experiment?
► Do you actively encourage experimentation when you co-facilitate?
► How do you use your co-facilitation to do this?
► What effect does your approach to experimentation seem to have on those groups with whom you work?
► Are there other ways in which you could use your co-facilitation to support experimentation?

Balancing challenge and support

Within the learning environment, there will undoubtedly be times when both challenge and support are appropriate in helping the group or particular group members to develop. Co-facilitators can offer greater flexibility here too. For example, if one facilitator has recently challenged the behaviour of a particular group member, then their co-facilitator may be better able to give any required support to that individual for a period following this intervention. The support may be received more easily. It may also be that, after making a particularly risky, difficult or tough intervention (however you might understand these terms), the facilitator needs or appreciates some support and reassurance from another professional and skilled facilitator regarding the appropriateness of their actions.

However, in saying this, it is important that one co-facilitator does not get labelled as the one who does all the hard and challenging work within the group, while the other is only perceived as offering comfort and support. This sort of labelling can be unhelpful for a number of reasons. If a male co-facilitator is seen as challenging, while their female co-facilitator is perceived as supportive, it can reinforce limited gender stereotypes which might inhibit the group's learning. Additionally, such one-dimensional co-facilitation can lead to challenge and support being perceived as mutually exclusive when, in our experience, making a strong challenge to an individual (which maybe other people in their lives have avoided making) can be a highly supportive thing to do – especially in the longer term. It is important, too, that learners do not feel that they are being asked to make a choice between being a challenging or a supportive person, when an alternative approach, of integrating these attributes and seeing them as complementary rather than contradictory, may be preferable.

The key, as mentioned before, is that co-facilitators should use their flexibility wisely and intentionally to help group members in their learning.

REFLECTION

▶ What has been the effect on you as a group member if co-facilitators have given noticeably different levels of challenge and support?

▶ When co-facilitating, do you typically offer support, challenge or similar amounts of each, as appropriate?

▶ What effect do you think your behaviour in this area has on the groups with which you work?

▶ Are there ways in which you could change, in order to enhance group members' learning?

▶ How might this affect the people with whom you most often co-facilitate?

Modelling

This brings us on to the usage of co-facilitator modelling, which we believe is one of the most significant benefits of co-facilitation. It can be an important indirect way of helping group members in their learning, supplementing more direct methods such as experiential exercises and activities, feedback and reflections on these, theoretical inputs and discussions about particular subjects or issues.

There are five main types of co-facilitator modelling, all of which we shall explore here.

1. Co-facilitators as representative of authority figures.
2. Co-facilitators as models of individuality not stereotypes.
3. Co-facilitators as models of effective interpersonal relationships.
4. Co-facilitators as models of good practice in specific areas.
5. Co-facilitators as models of professional practice in facilitation and co-facilitation.

Co-facilitators as representative of authority figures

Psychotherapeutic theory tells us that, when meeting or interacting with people, we are likely to transfer issues, feelings and behaviours about people in our past, whom we perceive to be similar, into the current situation. This has the effect of stopping us from responding fully to the current situation, because our reactions are influenced by these past situations. Co-facilitators, as perceived authority or leadership figures, may attract significant levels of transference from group members. They may transfer previous feelings about important authority figures from their past, such as parents and teachers, into the current situation. In this way, they are not responding fully to the co-facilitators themselves, but to past authority figures whom they may have perceived as good or bad, approachable or frightening, enabling or constraining etc. It is not necessary for the co-facilitators to behave in particular ways to attract this transference; it may be that something about their appearance is sufficient to trigger a transferential reaction. Male–female co-facilitative partnerships may attract particularly high levels of transference, by reminding group members of the first authority figures in their lives, that is their parents. Some group members may then start to react *as if* the co-facilitators were their parents rather than quite different individuals.

While individual facilitators will provoke transferential reactions, they may not be so strong or frequent as those provoked by co-facilitators where there is more opportunity of echoes from the past (from there being more than one person) and, particularly, echoes of probably the most influential people in our lives – our parents. These higher levels of transference can provide valuable learning opportunities, whether the transference is explored and worked through directly and overtly by co-facilitators with a psychotherapeutic bias in their work, or whether it is addressed indirectly by those who may lack the skill, knowledge or inclination – or perceive it to be inappropriate – to raise such issues overtly. For example, we may not label a response as transferential, although we might discuss the apparent difficulty experienced by a particular group member in dealing effectively with authority figures.

As well as increasing the possibility of transference, working with a co-facilitator also offers the opportunity for one co-facilitator to step back and be more objective, or perceived as being more objective, about analysing the interaction between their partner and a particular group member when this seems to be affected by transference. Their interpretation may therefore be more readily accepted by the group member involved and thus there may be greater learning for them as a result. A co-facilitator may also notice when a group member provokes a transferential reaction from their colleague, since such responses are not confined to group members! They can then provide support and practical help in working the issues through, so that the colleague can respond more appropriately to that individual.

There are many opportunities for learning to be gained from the exploration of such reactions by group members. Co-facilitators may learn that there is something in their manner, for example, which tends to provoke a consistent transferential response. They can then choose whether or not to change that and how to utilize its potential for group members' learning. Similarly, if a co-facilitator becomes aware that a group member is not directly responding to their partner, but seems to be reacting as if they were someone else or in another situation, then they can draw attention to this and help to assess and maybe change what is going on.

REFLECTION

▶ Are there any particular first impressions you seem to evoke in group members when you are facilitating? How do they typically see you?

▶ What (if anything) do you think you do, say and so on to create this reaction?

▶ Have group members ever said that you remind them of someone, for example, a mother/father, teacher or sister/brother? What were the similarities between you and these others?

▶ Do you believe that you tend to attract strong transference? How do you respond to this?

▶ How do you think that your co-facilitator could help you in using transference for your own and group members' learning?

▶ What have you learnt from this reflection?

We have found that one useful way of helping to identify the transference in a group, is to ask a group member to sculpt the group as if it were a family. By this, we mean that one member places individuals in family roles, positions and postures which reflect their own perception of:

● that person's relationship with other group members;
● that person's character, role and typical behaviour within the group.

It is important that the person who is sculpting the group remembers to include themselves in their sculpt, as this will indicate how they feel about their relationships with other group members. We believe it is also important that co-facilitators include themselves as part of the sculpt or they will lose a valuable source of feedback about their roles in this group. It is useful if the group member who has conducted the sculpt then explains, but not justifies, their perception to the others involved – or there is a chance that the significance which they attribute to a particular family member, the spacing between certain relations or the posture which participants were asked to adopt may well be missed.

There is no one truth about a group as each member will see it somewhat differently, so different group members can be asked to sculpt the group until it is felt that sufficient value has been taken from the exercise. Although some groups may find the concept of sculpting themselves as a family initially quite peculiar or threatening, our experience is that, once engaged in the activity, the majority of people and groups find it a very valuable and interesting way of learning about themselves. Figure 8.2 gives an example of what such a sculpt might look like.

The modelling the co-facilitators have embodied here, as parental figures, is not necessarily the result of any particular actions from them. It may be an unconscious response from group members to them, though this does not preclude the co-facilitators from making conscious use of it in contributing to the group's learning. However, there are other types of modelling which are more obvious manifestations of the co-facilitators themselves and which can also be used to aid group learning.

Co-facilitators as models of individuality not stereotypes

Some of these derive from the differences between co-facilitators, in terms of, for example, age, background, gender, sexual orientation and race. We have already referred to the potential danger of co-facilitators (or facilitators) reinforcing narrow stereotypes by their behaviour. However, they can also be powerful models of thinking, behaviour and attitudes outside of these stereotypes, which encourages group members to re-evaluate their usefulness. For example, if we take a commonly held stereotype, that women are less aggressive than men and tend to be more nurturing, this can effectively be challenged as a limiting definition of what is male and female by ensuring that a female co-facilitator does not undertake all the supportive interventions and, in addition, makes some confronting interventions where appropriate. It could also mean that the female co-facilitator adopts a high profile leadership role at significant times in the groupwork, such as at the beginning of the workshop or programme, which might subliminally start to overturn any stereotypical expectations about the roles which male and female co-facilitators will play.

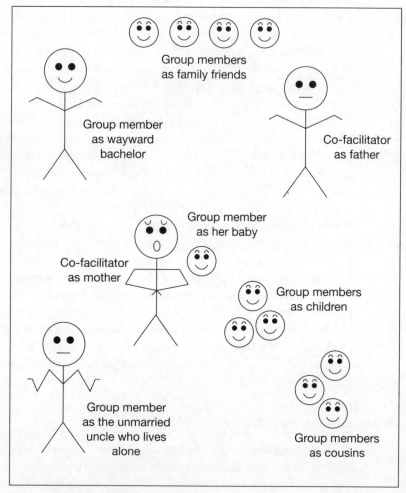

Figure 8.2 Group sculpt as family

Such challenging of stereotypes does not mean replacing one form of limitation with another, but requires exploration of the basis of stereotypes and assessment of their usefulness in interpersonal relations. It is important that, wherever possible, co-facilitators present themselves as having attributes and abilities which go beyond the limitations of the stereotype. This can have the effect of giving permission for group members to show and develop aspects of themselves, which perhaps they have felt unable to show to date, which fall outside of the conventional stereotypes. Supporting group members in extending their repertoire of behaviour, thinking and actions is likely to be valuable in enabling their growth and learning, and, therefore, in meeting the primary aim of most groupwork.

REFLECTION

▶ Do you represent any stereotypes as a co-facilitator? If so, what do you think you represent to the groups you work with?

▶ In what ways are you typical/untypical of particular stereotypes?

▶ Think of someone with whom you often co-facilitate. What stereotypes might they represent to group members?

▶ How could you use this to promote group learning?

▶ Is there anything you want to do differently as a result of this reflection?

Co-facilitators as models of effective interpersonal relationships

A different kind of modelling is also important in co-facilitation. This focuses on the overall quality of the interaction which occurs between the co-facilitators, and the nature of their relationship. This type of modelling is especially valuable in group situations where the main focus of development is on effective interpersonal relationships. Here, the co-facilitators can usefully model how to deal effectively with potentially difficult situations, such as disagreement or conflict, without this proving to be detrimental to their working relationship. While such situations should not be created in a manipulative way, when they arise they can provide a useful opportunity for a group to experience and study positive and powerful ways of dealing with potentially difficult interactions, and to notice their effects on those involved. This often contrasts with the unskilled and inappropriate handling of, for example, conflict situations which tends to be the norm in many organizations. Co-facilitators can also model effective teamwork in their way of working together, demonstrating how different skills and attributes can jointly contribute to the achievement of objectives. Again, this can send an important message to group members who may feel that individuality has to be submerged in order to promote effective teamwork. Although co-facilitators need to be alert to the benefits of such modelling in order to utilize it most effectively for group members' learning, they do not need to change their behaviour – providing that it naturally reflects appropriate interpersonal behaviour. This is an area on which they can usefully focus their mutual feedback since, to have credibility and validity as facilitators, we believe that it is important to practise what you preach – or, at least, since we are all fallible human beings, to aim to do this!

REFLECTION

▶ Have you experienced this kind of co-facilitator modelling when you were a group member? What effect did it have on you and your learning?

▶ Consider one person with whom you co-facilitate. In what ways do you demonstrate aspects of effective interpersonal relationships?

▶ Are there ways in which you might be demonstrating ineffective relationships?

▶ How could you improve your use of this kind of co-facilitator modelling?

Co-facilitators as models of good practice in specific areas

Co-facilitators can also offer another form of modelling which focuses attention on good practice in interpersonal relationships, and can help group members in identifying the gap between their current and desired practice. Depending on the issues being explored and addressed by the group as part of their development, the co-facilitators can set up and enact a situation which demonstrates to the group some aspects of effective practice in this area. For example, this can be used to demonstrate good counselling, appraisal, feedback or coaching skills, among others. While it is important to highlight the fact that there is no one right approach (otherwise group members may develop as clones of the co-facilitators!), this type of enactment can usefully show what is appropriate given particular responses and behaviours in a specific situation. This can act as a prompt for discussing what are likely to be effective or ineffective actions and behaviours in particular circumstances. It can be particularly useful when group members are currently at a fairly low level of competence in the area under review, so have no concept of what effective practice would look like.

Although this type of enactment can take place between a facilitator and a group member, it can prove difficult to demonstrate a high level of competence in a relatively short period of time if someone does not respond in expected ways – and there are no guarantees of this! We can never be fully responsible for another person's response, although we can hope to influence it by our own behaviour and actions. It can therefore be more helpful to model such situations with a co-facilitator, whom you know is likely to respond appopriately (and reasonably predictably) to your interventions.

REFLECTION

▶ What effect do you think this kind of co-facilitator modelling might have on group members' learning?
▶ What might stop you from using this kind of modelling in your co-facilitation?
▶ How could you try to get most benefit from this kind of modelling to aid group members' learning?
▶ Is there anything you will do differently as a result of this reflection?

Co-facilitators as models of professional practice in facilitation and co-facilitation

Finally, co-facilitators can model professional and personal effectiveness as both facilitators and as co-facilitators. Developing their practice in this specific area may be the particular purpose of the group's learning. For example, we work with many groups of trainers, developers, internal and external consultants, human resources managers and other line managers who, for various reasons, all want to improve their effectiveness as facilitators, and where this is the primary focus of the group and its development work. When co-facilitating, because of the obvious fact that there is more than one of you, you are able to model different ways of being effective, and so encourage group members in identifying and finding their own personal route to effectiveness in this role. You can also, as referred to earlier, demonstrate how good facilitators can work well together, by the quality of your relationship and the specific interactions which constitute it. In this way, you can also model effective co-facilitation. Since our research has shown that a fair proportion of facilitators have experienced ineffective co-facilitative relationships, such positive modelling is likely to be useful.

We hope that this review of co-facilitator modelling has demonstrated its importance as a benefit of co-facilitating and that it will encourage you to utilize your own co-facilitation in at least some of these ways.

SUMMARY

This chapter has attempted to redress, albeit briefly, the imbalance created by focusing on the relationship between co-facilitators rather than their relationship with the groups and individuals with whom they work. We have explored some ways in which the dynamics of the relationship between the co-facilitators and their groups can be surfaced and analysed, so that decisions can then be made about whether to maintain or change the style of the co-facilitation under review. These simple action enquiry methods should therefore help co-facilitators to enhance their effectiveness in supporting group members' learning. However, we have also cautioned that no one source of data should be used in isolation as this may lead to unbalanced analysis and inappropriate decisions.

We have also explored some of the particular purposes of co-facilitation, as compared to facilitation, within the overall umbrella of enabling group members' learning. Major ways in which co-facilitation can enhance learning are in furthering opportunities for group members to experiment, in providing alternative sources of challenge and support so that these interventions can be used more flexibly and in modelling effective behaviours which group members can then copy in their own way. We stress that the key here is flexibility – otherwise co-facilitators may fall into the trap of showing that there is one best way of doing things which, we believe, is a gross over-simplification of the reality of experience. Conversely, it is often the very complexity of work, business and relationships which co-facilitators are engaged in helping group members to recognize and deal with effectively. We hope that you are interested to find out as much as you can about how groups and individuals within them experience your co-facilitation. We also hope that you will remember the recipients of your work in any reviews which you engage in with your co-facilitator, so that your relationship with them never becomes an end in itself. That, as they say, is another story!

9

Conclusion

In this final chapter we want to emphasize what we have tried to achieve in writing this book. Our main aim has been to put the focus on co-facilitation for the first time and, in doing so, to address its taken-for-granted nature. We hope that we have been successful in encouraging you to think more deeply about your own co-facilitation and to consider ways in which you can actively work to enhance this in future.

We have attempted to aid your reflections in a number of ways. To this end, we have examined the potential benefits of co-facilitating compared with facilitating groupwork alone. While we are not suggesting that co-facilitation is appropriate for every piece of work, we believe that it can provide added value in many situations. Some of the most important benefits to be gained from co-facilitating are:

- enhanced development opportunities for the co-facilitators themselves;
- increased opportunities for group members' learning, particularly from co-facilitator modelling of desirable behaviours, attitudes and relationships;
- the bringing of complementary skills, styles and experiences to the group;
- the provision of support for the co-facilitators concerned.

We have tried to emphasize the key importance of the quality of the relationship between co-facilitators in achieving effective co-facilitation, that is, work which delivers high quality outcomes for client groups. Co-facilitators themselves have acknowledged its importance and we have provided some activities, frameworks and guides to reflection that will contribute to the improvement of the effectiveness of your co-facilitative relationships.

One key factor in the achievement of a good working relationship between co-facilitators is the level of awareness that informs their thinking, behaviours and actions. This awareness needs to have a broad focus, covering:

- yourself;
- your co-facilitator(s);
- the interplay between co-facilitators;
- the client group and individuals within it;
- the dynamics between group members;
- the interaction between co-facilitators and the group;
- the interaction between co-facilitators and individual group members;
- the wider working environment;
- the objectives of the particular work being undertaken.

Without good levels of co-facilitator awareness, certain issues may be ignored rather than recognized and addressed. These may then act to limit the effectiveness of the relationship between the co-facilitators and of their work with client groups.

To support the development of this awareness we have identified some of the main dynamics found to occur in co-facilitative relationships. We hope that this helps you to become aware of the issues that may arise in your co-facilitative relationships. Sometimes being aware of the potentially difficult dynamics that might arise between co-facilitators can help you to avoid them – and developing clear working contracts with new co-facilitators can certainly help too. When these issues are not recognized and therefore not subsequently addressed, they are likely to impact adversely on the relationship between the co-facilitators.

However, being aware of issues is not, of itself, enough. This awareness needs to inform action on the part of the co-facilitators to resolve any potentially unproductive issues. In order to achieve this resolution, co-facilitators require certain skills such as:

- confronting, rather than ignoring, issues;
- conflict handling;
- giving and receiving feedback;
- self-disclosure;
- giving and receiving support;
- a learning orientation.

When issues can be worked through by the co-facilitators involved by using skills such as those identified above, increased opportunities for their learning and development occur. You can utilize the exercises and activities provided, particularly those in Chapters 3, 4 and 6, to develop these skills and to help you in taking practical steps to enhance your co-facilitative relationships.

We have also given examples of various different working contracts to encourage you to set out how you want to work with particular co-facilitators from the start of your working relationship. However, you should be aware of the likely need periodically to renegotiate your working contract to take account of changes in your relationship. This sort of renegotiation can also prompt an in-depth review of how your relationship is currently working. It is helpful if difficulties arising between co-facilitators are not seen as signs of failure, but as opportunities for learning.

We have also explored the impact of the co-facilitative relationship on the client groups with whom the co-facilitators work. In focusing primarily on the importance of the relationship between co-facilitators, we are conscious that there is a danger of encouraging an inward rather than an outward looking approach. This is not our intention. We have focused on the relationship because we believe that paying attention to this is critical in delivering the best quality learning for client groups. In the same way a good car will get you to your destination more quickly, in greater comfort and safety, and with you feeling more refreshed than travelling in an old banger. Even good and reliable cars need regular servicing. We would encourage you to explore the links between your own co-facilitative relationships and the results which you achieve with groups, in order to test further the validity of our theory.

We have learnt a lot from writing this book, from reflecting on our own co-facilitative practice and from carrying out the research on which our writing has been based. We have become increasingly aware of how we as co-facilitators can help to create the appropriate environment for the development of an effective working relationship and how we can take responsibility for progressing this. One key way of doing this is by the creation of a learning orientation as the framework for the co-facilitative relationship, which then influences the way in which reviews and feedback are handled. Importantly, this orientation is highly congruent with the type of work undertaken by co-facilitators. We are convinced that our ability to continue to push out our boundaries in facilitation is helped and supported by working with highly skilled co-facilitators, and we shall continue to look for opportunities to do this.

The process of working together to write this book has, in some ways, been similar to co-facilitating. While there have been periods of frustration, arising from the practical difficulties in getting together because of work pressures and changing personal circumstances, the final product has benefited from the synergy that has resulted from working together. We have been able to experiment with different ways of producing the written material, and have learnt from this process. We have been able to support each other through the research and production, helping one another to sustain motivation and commitment through some particularly hectic work periods and times of considerable personal upheaval. At times it has been this level of commitment to each other that has kept us going – without it there might not have been a book. We believe, therefore, that in a different context we have been able to access some of the most important advantages of co-facilitating.

Conducting this research and writing this book has also confirmed our interest in developing others who work in this field – as trainers, developers, facilitators, internal or external consultants of different types – work that already forms a significant part of our consultancy activity. We believe that those of us who work in this area need to be particularly mindful of our responsibility to develop ourselves, both personally and professionally, to ensure that we develop and maintain high levels of competence, since we often exert considerable influence on large numbers of individuals and the sizeable organizations which employ them. It is important that we exercise our influence with responsibility, and this book is an attempt to help in this process.

But we have only just started, rather than finished, our exploration into this topic. The end point of any research is almost inevitably an arbitrary one and our research will continue beyond the arbitrary point represented by the publication of this book. We therefore invite you to send us any reflections on your own co-facilitative experiences, good and bad, which you would like to share with us, and which we could incorporate into any future updates of this book, and into our development work with facilitators and consultants.

Finally, we wish you well in your future co-facilitation. We hope that you can create some true partnerships and that, if you do encounter some difficulties, this book will act as a useful prompt and guide for you in tackling them successfully.

Bibliography

Barber, P (1994) *An Experiential Exploration of Stress in Group Settings*, Human Potential Resource Group, University of Surrey.

Berry, M (1993) 'Changing Perspectives on Facilitation Skills Development', *Journal of European Industrial Training*, 17, 3, 23–32.

Burgess, R G (1982) *Field Research: A sourcebook and field manual*, Allen & Unwin, London.

Corey, M S and Corey, G (1992) *Groups Process and Practice*, Brooks/Cole Publishing Company, Pacific Grove, California.

Easterby Smith, M, Thorpe, R and Lowe, A (1991) *Management Research*, Sage, London.

Gately, F and Gately, S (1993) Developing Positive Co-teaching Environments: Meeting the needs of an increasingly diverse student population', paper presented at the Annual Meeting of the Council for Exceptional Children, San Antonio, USA.

Gill, J and Johnson, P (1991) *Research Methods for Managers*, Paul Chapman Publishing, London.

Heron, J (1989) *The Facilitator's Handbook*, Kogan Page, London.

Houston, G (1993) *The Red Book of Gestalt*, The Rochester Foundation, London.

Karpman, S (1968) 'Fairy Tales and Script Analysis', *Transactional Analysis Bulletin*, 7, 39–43.

Karpman, S (1971) 'Options', *Transactional Analysis Journal*, 1, 79–87.

Knight, S (1995) *NLP at Work*, NB Publishing, London.

Maclean, H (1988) 'Linking Person-Centred Teaching to Qualitative Research Training', in *Appreciating Adults Learning: From the Learner's Perspective*, D Boud and V Griffin (eds), Kogan Page, London.

Scott, W (1994) *Co-facilitation: A marriage of rivers*, Surrey University.

Spinks, T and Clements, P (1993) *A Practical Guide to Facilitation Skills: A Real World Approach*, Kogan Page, London.

Stewart, I and Joines, V (1989) *TA Today*, Sage, London.

Index